The Art of Life

The Art of Life

Zygmunt Bauman

polity

First published in 2008 by Polity Press
Reprinted 2009, 2010

Polity Press
65 Bridge Street
Cambridge CB2 1UR, UK.

Polity Press
350 Main Street
Malden, MA 02148, USA.

ISBN-13: 978-0-7456-4325-0
ISBN-13: 978-0-7456-4326-7 (pb)

A catalogue record for this book is available from the British Library.

Typeset in 11 on 13 pt Sabon
by SNP Best-set Typesetter Ltd., Hong Kong
Printed and bound in Great Britain by MPG Books, Bodmin, Cornwall

For further information on Polity, visit our website: www.politybooks.com

Contents

You are not an isolated entity,
but a unique, irreplaceable part of the cosmos.
Don't forget this.
You are an essential piece in the puzzle of humanity.

Epictetus, *The Art of Living*

It is the wish of all men . . . to live happily,
but when it comes to seeing clearly what it is that makes life happy,
they grope for the light;
indeed, a measure of the difficulty of achieving the happy life
is that the greater the man's energy in striving for it,
the further he goes away from it
if he has taken a wrong turning on the road . . .

Seneca, 'On the happy life'

INTRODUCTION
What is Wrong with Happiness?

The question in the title would baffle many a reader. And it is meant to baffle – to prompt one to pause and think. To pause in what? In our pursuit of happiness, which – as most readers would probably agree – is on our minds most of the time, fills the greater part of our lives, cannot and will not slow down, let alone stop . . . at least no longer than for a (fleeting, always fleeting) moment.

Why is this question likely to baffle? Because to ask 'what is wrong with happiness?' is like asking what is hot about ice or malodorous in a rose. Ice being incompatible with heat, and rose with stench, such questions assume the feasibility of an *inconceivable* coexistence (where there is heat, there can't be ice). How, indeed, could something be *wrong* with *happiness*? Is not 'happiness' a synonym of the *absence* of wrong? Of the very *impossibility* of its presence? Of the impossibility of *all and any* wrong?!

And yet this is a question asked by Michael Rustin,[1] as it has been by quite a few worried people before and probably will be in the future – and Rustin explains why: societies like ours, moved by millions of men and women pursuing happiness, are getting richer, but it is far from clear whether they are getting happier. It looks as if the human pursuit of happiness may well prove to be self-defeating. All the available empirical data suggest that among the populations of affluent societies there may be no connection

at all between rising affluence, believed to be the principal vehicle
of a happy life, and greater happiness!

The close correlation between economic growth and enhanced
happiness is widely believed to be one of the least questionable
truths, perhaps even the most self-evident. Or at least, this is what
the best-known and most respected political leaders, their advisers
and spokespeople, tell us – and what we, who tend to rely on their
opinions, repeat without pause for reflection or second thoughts.
They and we act on the assumption that the correlation is genuine.
We want them to act on that belief still more resolutely and ener-
getically – and we wish them luck, hoping that their success (that
is, adding to our incomes, to our disposable cash, to the volume
of our possessions, assets and wealth) will add quality to our lives
and make us feel happier than we are.

According to virtually all the research reports scrutinized and
summed up by Rustin, 'improvements in living standards in
nations such as the United States and Britain are associated with
no improvement – indeed a slight decline – in subjective well-
being.' Robert Lane has found that despite the massive, spectacular rise of American incomes in the postwar years, the self-reported
happiness of Americans has declined.[2] And Richard Layard has
concluded from a cross-national comparison of data that although
the indices of reported satisfaction with life grow by and large in
parallel with the level of national product, they rise significantly
only up to the point where want and poverty give way to the
gratification of essential, 'survival' needs – and stop climbing or
tend to slow down drastically with further rises in affluence.[3] On
the whole, only a few percentage points separate countries with
an average annual income per capita between 20,000 and 35,000
dollars from those below the barrier of 10,000 dollars. The strategy of making people happier through raising their income does
not seem to work. On the other hand, one social index that seems
to be growing most spectacularly in line with the level of affluence, indeed as fast as subjective well-being was promised and
expected to rise, has so far been the incidence of criminality: of
burglary and car theft, drug trafficking, economic graft and business corruption. And of an uncomfortable and uneasy sensation
of uncertainty, hard to bear, let alone to live with permanently.
Of a diffuse and 'ambient' uncertainty, ubiquitous yet seemingly
unanchored, unspecified and for that reason all the more vexing
and aggravating . . .

Such findings feel profoundly disappointing, considering that it was precisely an increase in the overall volume of happiness 'of the greatest number' – an increase led by economic growth and a rise in disposable cash and credit – that was declared, through the last several decades, to be the main purpose guiding the policies set by our governments, as well as the 'life politics' strategies of our, their subjects. It also served as the main yardstick for measuring the success and failure of governmental policies, and of our pursuit of happiness. We could even say that our modern era started in earnest with the proclamation of the universal human right to the pursuit of happiness, and from the promise to demonstrate its superiority over the forms of life it replaced by rendering that pursuit less cumbersome and arduous, while being more effective. We may ask, then, whether the means suggested to achieve such a demonstration (principally, continuous economic growth as measured by the rise in 'gross national product') were wrongly chosen? If so, what exactly was wrong with that choice?

The sole common denominator of the otherwise variegated products of human bodily and mental labour being the market price they command, the statistics of the 'gross national product' aimed at grasping the growth or decline of the products' availability record the amount of money changing hands in the course of buying and selling transactions. Whether or not the indices of GNP acquit themselves well in their overt task, there is still a question of whether they should be treated, as they tend to be, as indicators of the growth or decline of happiness. It is assumed that as the spending of money goes up, it must coincide with a similar upward movement in the happiness of spenders, but this is not immediately obvious. If, for instance, the pursuit of happiness as such, known to be an absorbing, energy-consuming, risk-fraught and nerve-taxing activity, leads to a greater incidence of mental depression, more money is likely to be spent on anti-depressants. If, thanks to an increase in car ownership, the frequency of car accidents and the number of accident victims grow, so too does expenditure on car repairs and medical treatment. If the quality of tap-water goes on deteriorating all over the place, more and more money will be spent on buying bottled water to be carried in our rucksacks or travel bags on all trips, long or short (we will be asked to swill the contents of the bottle on the spot whenever we approach this side of the airport security check, and need to buy another bottle on the other side of the checkpoint).

In all such cases, and a multitude of similar instances, more money changes hands, boosting the GNP figures. This is certain. But a parallel growth in the happiness of consumers of anti-depressants, victims of car accidents, carriers of water bottles, and, indeed, of all those many people who worry about bad luck and fear their turn to suffer might come – that is far less obvious.

All that should not really be news. As Jean-Claude Michéa recalled recently in his timely rewriting of the convoluted history of the 'modern project',[4] as long ago as 18 March 1968, in the heat of the presidential campaign, Robert Kennedy launched a scathing attack on the lie on which the GNP-bound measure of happiness rests:

> Our GNP takes into account in its calculations the air pollution, tobacco advertising and ambulances riding to collect the wounded from our motorways. It registers the costs of the security systems which we install to protect our homes and the prisons in which we lock up those who manage to break into them. It entails the destruction of our sequoia forests and their replacement through sprawling and chaotic urbanization. It includes the production of napalm, nuclear arms and armed vehicles used by police to stifle urban unrest. It records ... television programmes that glorify violence in order to sell toys to children. On the other hand, GNP does not note the health of our children, quality of our education or gaiety of our games. It does not measure the beauty of our poetry and the strength of our marriages. It does not care to evaluate the quality of our political debates and integrity of our representatives. It leaves out of consideration our courage, wisdom and culture. It says nothing about our compassion and dedication to our country. In a word, the GNP measures everything, except what makes life worth the pain of living it.

Robert Kennedy was murdered a few weeks after publishing this fiery indictment and declaring his intention to restore the importance of things that make life worth living; so we will never know whether he would have tried, let alone succeeded, in making his words flesh had he been elected President of the United States. What we do know, though, is that in the forty years that have passed since, there have been few if any signs of his message having been heard, understood, embraced and remembered – let alone any move on the part of our elected representatives to disown and repudiate the pretence of the commodity markets to the role of the royal road to a meaningful and happy life, or evidence of any inclination on our part to reshape our life strategies accordingly.

Observers suggest that about half the goods crucial for human happiness have no market price and can't be purchased in shops. Whatever your cash and credit standing, you won't find in a shopping mall love and friendship, the pleasures of domesticity, the satisfaction that comes from caring for loved ones or helping a neighbour in distress, the self-esteem to be drawn from work well done, gratifying the 'workmanship instinct' common to us all, the appreciation, sympathy and respect of workmates and other people with whom one associates; you won't find there freedom from the threats of disregard, contempt, snubs and humiliation. Moreover, earning enough money to afford those goods that can only be had through the shops is a heavy tax on the time and energy available to obtain and enjoy *non*-commercial and *non*-marketable goods like the ones listed above. It may easily happen, and frequently does, that the losses exceed the gains and the capacity of increased income to generate happiness is overtaken by the unhappiness caused by a shrinking access to the goods which 'money can't buy'.

Consumption takes time (as does shopping), and the sellers of consumer goods are naturally interested in tapering to a bare minimum the time dedicated to the enjoyable act of consuming. Simultaneously, they are interested in cutting down as far as possible, or eliminating altogether, those necessary activities that occupy much time but bring few marketing profits. In view of their frequency in commercial catalogues, promises in the descriptions of the new products on offer – like 'absolutely no effort required', 'no skills called for', 'you will enjoy [music, views, delights of the palate, the restored cleanliness of your blouse etc.] in minutes' or 'in just one touch' – seem to assume a convergence in the interests of sellers and buyers. Promises like these are covert/oblique admissions that the sellers of goods would not wish their buyers to spend too much time enjoying them, so wasting time that could be used for more shopping escapades – but evidently they must also be a very reliable selling point. It must have been found that prospective customers wish for quick results and only a momentary engagement of their mental and physical faculties – probably to vacate time for more attractive alternatives. If cans can be opened with a less 'bad for you' kind of effort thanks to a new miraculously ingenious electronic can-opener, more time will be left to spend in a gym exercising with gadgets promising a 'good for you' variety of exertion. But whatever the gains in such an exchange, their impact on the sum total of happiness is anything but unambiguous.

Laura Potter embarked on her ingenious exploration of all sorts of waiting rooms expecting that she would find there 'impatient, disgruntled, red-faced people cursing each lost millisecond' – fulminating at the need to wait for whatever 'urgent business' brought them there.[5] With our 'cult of instant gratification', she mused, many of us would 'have lost the ability to wait':

> We live in an era where 'waiting' has become a dirty word. We've gradually eradicated (as much as possible) the need to wait for anything, and our new, up-to-the-second adjective is 'instant'. We can no longer spare a meagre 12 minutes for a pan of rice to boil, so a time-saving two-minute microwavable version has been created. We can't be bothered to wait for Mr or Mrs Right to come along, so we speed date . . . In our time-pressed lives, it seems that the 21st-century Briton no longer has time to wait for anything.

Much to her surprise (and perhaps that of most of us), however, Laura Potter found a very different picture. Wherever she went, she sensed the same feeling: 'the wait was a pleasure . . . Waiting seemed to have become a luxury, a window in our tightly scheduled lives. In our "now" culture of BlackBerrys, laptops and mobile phones, "waitees" viewed the waiting room as a place of refuge.' Perhaps the waiting room, Potter concludes, reminds us of the intensely pleasurable, alas forgotten, art of relaxing . . .

The pleasures of relaxation are not the only ones to have been laid at the altar of a life hurried for the sake of saving time to chase other things. When the effects that were once attained thanks to our own ingenuity, dedication and hard-learned skills are 'outsourced' to a gadget requiring only a swish of a credit card and a push of a button, something that used to make many people happy and was probably vital for everybody's happiness is lost on the way: pride in 'work well done', in dexterity, smartness and skill, in a daunting task performed, an indomitable obstacle overcome. In the longer run, skills once obtained, and the very ability to learn and master new skills, are forgotten and lost, and with them goes the joy of gratifying the workmanship instinct, that vital condition of self-esteem, so difficult to replace, along with the happiness offered by self-respect.

The markets, to be sure, are keen to redress the harm done – with the help of factory-made substitutes for the 'do-it-yourself' goods that can no longer be 'done by yourself' because of your lack of time and vigour. Following the market's suggestion and using its (paid-up and profit-generating) services, one would for instance invite a partner to a restaurant, treat children to McDonald's burgers, or bring home takeaways instead of preparing meals 'from scratch' in the family kitchen; or one would purchase expensive gifts for loved ones to compensate for the dearth of time spent together and the rarity of the occasions to talk to each other, as well as for the absence or near absence of convincing manifestations of personal interest, compassion and care. Even the agreeable taste of the restaurant food or the high price tags and highly prestigious labels attached to the gifts sold in the shops will, however, hardly match up to the value in added happiness of the goods for whose absence or rarity they are meant to compensate: such goods as gathering around a table laid with food that has been jointly cooked with its sharing in mind, or lengthy, attentive listening by a person-who-counts to one's intimate thoughts, hopes and apprehensions, and similar proofs of loving attention, engagement and care. Since not all goods necessary for 'subjective happiness', and notably the non-marketable goods, have a common denominator, their balances elude quantification; no increase in the quantity of one good can fully and truly compensate for the lack of a good of a different quality and provenance.

All and any offerings call for a certain sacrifice on the part of the giver, and it is precisely the awareness of self-sacrifice that adds to the giver's feeling of happiness. Gifts that take no effort and call for no sacrifice, and therefore do not require resignation from some other coveted values, are worthless in this respect. The great humanist psychologist Abraham Maslow and his little son shared their love of strawberries. Their wife and mother indulged them with strawberries for breakfast; 'my son', Maslow told me, 'was, as most children are, impatient, impetuous, unable to slowly savour his delights and stretch his joy for longer; he emptied his plate in no time, and then looked wistfully at mine, still almost full. Each time it happened, I passed my strawberries to him. And you know', so Maslow concluded the story, 'I remember those strawberries tasting better in his mouth than in mine . . .' Markets have flawlessly spotted the opportunity of capitalizing on the impulse to self-sacrifice, that faithful companion of love and friendship. The willingness to self-sacrifice has been commercialized, just like most other needs or desires whose gratification has been acknowledged as indispensable for human happiness (a Cassandra of our days would advise us to be wary of markets even when bringing gifts . . .). Self-sacrifice now means mostly, and preferably exclusively, parting with a large or possibly yet larger sum of money: an act that can be duly recorded in the GNP statistics.

To conclude: pretending that the volume and depth of human happiness can be taken care of and properly served by fixing attention on just one index – GNP – is grossly misleading. When it is made into a principle of governance, such a pretence may become harmful as well, bringing consequences opposite to those intended and allegedly pursued.

Once life-enhancing goods start to move from the non-monetary realm to the commodity market, there is no stopping them; the movement tends to develop its own momentum and becomes self-propelling and self-accelerating, diminishing yet further the supply of goods that by their nature can only be produced personally and can only flourish in the setting of intense and intimate human relationships. The less possible it is to offer to others goods of the latter kind, goods 'that money can't buy', or the less willingness there is to cooperate with others in their production (a willingness to cooperate is often greeted as the most satisfying good that can be offered), the deeper are the feelings of guilt and the unhappiness that result. A wish to atone and to redeem the guilt pushes the sinner to seek yet more expensive, buyable substitutes for what is no longer offered to the people with whom their life is lived, and so to spend yet more hours away from them in order to earn more money. The chance to produce and share the sorely missed goods which one is too busy and too exhausted to conjure up and to offer is thereby yet further impoverished.

It looks therefore as if the *growth of 'national product'* is a rather poor measure of the *growth of happiness*. It may be seen instead as a sensitive indicator of the strategies, wayward and misleading as they may be, which in our *pursuit* of happiness we have been forced, persuaded or cajoled to adopt – or manoeuvred into adopting. What we can learn from GNP statistics is how many of the routes followed by seekers of happiness have been already redesigned to lead through the shops, those prime sites for money to change hands – whether or not the strategies adopted by happiness-seekers differ in other ways (and they do differ), and whether or not the routes they suggest vary in other ways (and they do vary). We can deduce from those statistics how strong and how widespread is the *belief* that there is an intimate link between happiness and the volume and quality of consumption: an assumption that underlies all shop-mediated strategies. What we can also learn is how successfully markets manage to deploy that hidden assumption as a profit-churning engine – by identifying happiness-generating consumption with consumption of the objects and services offered for sale in the shops. At this point, marketing success rebounds as a sorry plight, and ultimately as an abominable failure of the self-same pursuit of happiness it had been presumed to serve.

One of the most seminal effects of equating happiness with shopping for commodities which are hoped to generate happiness is to stave off the chance that the pursuit of happiness will ever grind to a halt. The pursuit of happiness will never end – its end would be equal to the end of happiness as such. The secure *state* of happiness not being attainable, it is only the *chase* of that stubbornly elusive target that can keep the runners (however moderately) happy. On that track leading to happiness, there is no finishing line. The ostensible means turn into ends: the sole available consolation for the elusiveness of the dreamed-of and coveted 'state of happiness' is to stay on course; as long as one stays in the race, neither falling from exhaustion nor being shown a red card, the hope of eventual victory is kept alive.

By subtly shifting the dream of happiness from the vision of a full and fully gratifying life to the search for means believed to be needed for such a life to be reached, markets see to it that the pursuit can never end. The targets of the search replace each other with mind-boggling speed. It is fully understood by the pursuers (and, of course, by their zealous coaches and guides) that if the pursuit is to achieve its declared purpose, the pursued targets have to quickly fall out of use, lose their lustre, attraction and power of seduction, be abandoned and replaced – and many times over – by other, 'new and improved' targets, doomed to suffer a similar lot. Imperceptibly, the vision of happiness shifts from an anticipated *after-purchase* bliss to the act of *shopping* that precedes it – an act overflowing with joyous anticipation; joyous for a hope as yet pristine, untarnished and undashed.

Thanks to the diligence and expertise of the advertising copywriters, such life-and-(high)street wisdom tends nowadays to be acquired at a tender age, well before there is a first chance to hear subtle philosophical meditations on the nature of happiness and the ways to a happy life, let alone a chance to study them and reflect on their message. We may learn, for instance, from the first page of the 'Fashion' section of a widely read and well-respected magazine, that Liberty, a twelve-year-old schoolgirl, 'has already discovered how to make her wardrobe work well'.[6] Topshop is her 'favourite store', and for a good reason: in her own words, 'even though it's really expensive, I know that I'll come out with something fashionable.' What the frequent visits to Topshop mean for her is first and foremost a comforting feeling of safety: Topshop's buyers confront the risks of failure on her behalf and take the responsibility for the choice on themselves. Once she buys in that shop, the probability of making a mistake is reduced to nil, or almost. Liberty does not trust her own taste and discretion sufficiently to buy (let alone don in public) just what has caught her eye; but things she bought in that shop she can parade in public with confidence – confident of recognition, approval and, in the end, of the admiration and high status that closely follow it: all those feel-good things which parading clothes and accessories in public is intended to achieve. Says Liberty of the shorts she bought last January: 'I hated them. I did love them but then I got them home and I thought they were too short. But then I read *Vogue* and I saw this lady in shorts – and they were my shorts from Topshop! Ever since then I've been inseparable from them.' This is what the label, the logo, and the location can do for their customers: guide them on the confusingly twisted, booby-trapped road to happiness. The happiness of being issued with a publicly recognized and respected certificate confirming (authoritatively!) that one is on the right track, is still in the chase, and is allowed to keep one's hopes alive.

The snag is: how long will the certificate stay valid? You can bet that the 'ever since' of 'being inseparable', true as they were in April 2007, won't last long in Liberty's long life. The lady wearing short shorts will not appear in *Vogue* a few issues later. The certificate of public approval will reveal its small print and abominably brief validity span. You can even bet that on her next visit to Topshop Liberty will not find similar shorts – even if she, improbably, were to seek them. But you would be a hundred per cent sure to win if you bet that Liberty's visits to Topshop would continue. She will go there again and again. Why? First, she has learned to trust the wisdom of whoever in that shop decides what to put on the shelves and trolleys on the day of her visit; she trusts them to sell things complete with a guarantee of public approval and social recognition. Second, she knows already from her brief yet intense experience that what has been put on shelves and trolleys one day won't be there a few days later, and that to update the fast-ageing knowledge of what 'is (still) in' and what 'is (already) out' and to find out what is very much 'on' today, though it was not at all on display yesterday, one must visit the shop frequently enough to make sure that the wardrobe goes on 'working well' without interruption.

Unless you find a label, a logo, a shop you can trust, you are confused and may be lost. Labels, logos, shops are the few remaining safe havens amidst the ominous rapids that threaten your safety; the few shelters of certainty in a vexingly uncertain world. On the other hand, however, if you've invested your trust in a label, a logo, or a shop, you have mortgaged your future. The short-term certificates of 'being in' or 'up to date' will continue to be issued only as long as you keep your investment invested. And the people behind the label, the logo, or the shop will see to it that the timespan of the validity of the newly issued certificates will be no longer than the validity of the old ones, if not still shorter.

Obviously, mortgaging one's future is a serious business and a serious decision to take. Liberty is twelve years old and has a long future ahead, but however long or short one's future might be, pursuing happiness in a consumer-market society of labels, logos and shops *requires* that it be mortgaged. The celebrated actor featuring in a full-page advertisement of the Samsonite company is much older than Liberty, but his future seems similarly mortgaged; though, as is proper for his age, the mortgage contract was signed well in the past (or, at least, this is what the advertisement insinuates). The title of the advertising copy, 'Life's a journey', sets the stage for the bold type, partly capital-letters message: 'CHARACTER is all about retaining a strong IDENTITY' (note the 'retaining' bit). The celebrated actor, photographed in a boat sailing along the Seine with Notre Dame in the background, clutches the latest Samsonite product, a 'Graviton' suitcase (note the reference to 'gravity' in the name of a travelling accessory boasting of its lightness) – an image which the copywriters, lest it won't be fully digested, hasten to explain: the celebrated actor, they say, 'is making a statement as he travels with Samsonite Graviton'. They don't say anything about the contents of the statement, though. They hope, certainly not without reason, that to a seasoned reader the contents will be unambiguous without further explanation. The meaning of the statement will be easily grasped: 'I am returning from the John Lewis department store where Gravitons have just been put on sale. I've bought one in the company of other people with gravity, and so increased (retained?) a specific gravity of my own.'

For the celebrated actor, as for Liberty, having and displaying publicly things carrying the right label and/or logo and obtained in the right shop is primarily a matter of obtaining and retaining the *social standing* which they guard or to which they aspire. Social standing means nothing unless it has been socially *recognized*; that is, unless the person in question is approved by the right kind of 'society' (each category of social standing has its own proper codes of law and judges) as its rightful and deserving member – as 'one of us'.

Labels, logos and brands are the terms of the *language of recognition*. What is hoped to be and as a rule is to be 'recognized' with the help of brands and logos is what has been discussed in recent years under the name of *identity*. The operation described above stands behind the preoccupation with 'identity' accorded such centrality in our society of consumers. Showing 'character' and having one's 'identity' recognized, as well as finding and obtaining the means to assure the achievement of these interrelated purposes, become central preoccupations in the pursuit of a happy life.

Though it has remained an important issue and an absorbing task since the early modern passage from an 'ascription' to an 'achievement' society (that is, from a society in which people were 'born into' their identities, to a society in which construction of identity is their task and responsibility), 'identity' has now shared the fate of other life accoutrements: devoid of a direction determined once and for all, and no longer meant to leave behind solid and indestructible traces, identity is now expected and preferred to be easy to melt and suitable for recasting in moulds of different shapes. Once a 'whole life' project, identity has now turned into an attribute of the moment. Once designed, it is no longer 'built to last forever', but needs to be continuously *assembled* and *disassembled*. Each of those two apparently contradictory operations carries equal importance and tends to be equally absorbing.

Instead of demanding an advance payment and a lifelong subscription with no cancellation clause, the manipulation of identity is now an activity akin to the 'pay as you watch' (or 'as you phone') facility. It is still a constant preoccupation, but now split into a multitude of exceedingly short (and thanks to progress in marketing techniques, ever shorter) efforts, able to be absorbed by even the most fleeting attention; a succession of sudden and frenetic spurts of activity which is neither predesigned nor predictable, but has instead immediate effects that follow comfortably closely and do not threaten to outstay their welcome.

The skills required to meet the challenge of the liquid modern reprocessing and recycling manipulation of identity are akin to those of a juggler, or, more to the point, to the artfulness and dexterity of a prestidigitator. The practice of such skills has been brought within the reach of an ordinary, run-of-the-mill consumer by the expedient of *simulacrum* – a phenomenon (in the memorable description of Jean Baudrillard) similar to psychosomatic ailments, known to cancel the distinction between 'things as they are' and 'things as they pretend to be', between 'reality' and 'illusion', or between the 'true state' of affairs and its 'simulation'. What once was viewed and suffered as an interminable drudgery calling for uninterrupted mobilization and an onerous straining of every 'inner' resource, can now be accomplished with the help of purchasable, ready-to-use contraptions and gadgets with the expenditure of a modicum of money and time – though, of course, the attractiveness of an identity composed of bought trappings rises in proportion to the amount of money spent. Most recently it has begun to rise as well with length of waiting, as the most prestigious and exclusive designer shops introduce waiting lists – clearly for no other purpose than to enhance the distinction with which the waited-for tokens of identity endow their buyer. As Georg Simmel, one of the founding fathers of social science, pointed out a long time ago, values are measured by the other values which have to be sacrificed to obtain them, and delay in gratification is arguably the most excruciating of sacrifices for people cast in the fast-moving and fast-changing settings characteristic of our liquid modern society of consumers.

Annulling the past, 'being born again', acquiring a different and more attractive self while discarding the one that is old, worn out and no longer wanted, reincarnating as 'someone completely different' and starting from 'a new beginning' . . . such enticing offers are difficult to reject out of hand. Indeed, why work on self-improvement with all the strenuous effort and painful self-sacrifice such toil inevitably requires? And in the event that all that effort, self-denial and noxious austerity fails to make up for the losses soon enough – why send good money after bad? Is it not obvious that it is cheaper, and quicker, and more thorough, and more convenient, and easier to achieve, to cut your losses and start again – to shed the old skin, spots, warts and all, and buy a new one, ready-made and ready-to-wear?

There is nothing new in seeking escape when things get really hot; people have tried that, with mixed success, at all times. What is really new is the twin dream of *escaping from one's own self* and *acquiring a made-to-order self*; and a conviction that making such a dream a reality is within reach. Not just *an* option within reach, but the *easiest* option, the one most likely to work in case of trouble; a short-cut option, less cumbersome, less time-and-energy consuming and so all in all *cheaper* if measured, according to Simmel's advice, by the volume of the other values which have to be given up or curtailed.

If happiness is permanently within reach, and if reaching it takes only the few minutes needed to browse through the yellow pages and pull a credit card out of a wallet, then obviously a self that stops short of reaching happiness can't be 'real' or 'genuine', but a relic of sloth, ignorance or ineptitude – if not all of them together. Such a self must be counterfeit or fraudulent. The absence of happiness, or insufficient happiness, or happiness less intense than the kind proclaimed as attainable to all who tried hard enough and used the proper means with proper skills, is all the reason one needs to refuse to settle for the 'self' one has and to embark and continue on a voyage of self-discovery (or rather self-invention). Fraudulent or botched selves need to be discarded on the grounds of their 'non-authenticity', while the search for the real one should go on. And there is little reason to stop searching if one can be sure that in a short moment the moment being lived will become history and another moment will duly arrive, carrying new promises, bursting with new potential, auguring a new beginning . . .

In a society of shoppers and a life of shopping *we are happy as long as we haven't lost the hope of becoming happy*; we are secure from unhappiness as long as some of that hope is still ticking. And so the key to happiness and the antidote to misery is to keep the hope of becoming happy *alive*. But it can stay alive only on condition of a rapid succession of 'new chances' and 'new beginnings', and of the prospect of an infinitely long chain of new starts ahead. That condition is brought about by slicing life into episodes: that is, into preferably self-enclosed and self-contained time stretches, each with its own plot, its own characters and its own ending. The latter requisite – the ending – is met if the characters acting or acted upon in the course of the episode are presumed to be engaged solely for its duration, with no commitment made as to their admission to the episode which follows. Each episode having its own plot, each needs a new casting. Any indefinite, interminable commitment would severely limit the range of plots available for the succeeding episodes. An indefinite commitment and the pursuit of happiness seem to be at cross-purposes. In a society of consumers all ties and bonds have to follow the pattern of the relationship between buyer and commodities bought: commodities are not expected to outstay their welcome and must leave the stage of life once they start to clutter it up instead of adorning it, whereas buyers are neither expected nor willing to swear eternal loyalty to the purchases they bring home or to grant them permanent rights of residence. Relationships of the consumerist type are, from the start, 'until further notice'.

In a recent survey of the new types of relationships tending to replace the old 'till death us do part' kind, Stuart Jeffries notes the rising tide of 'commitment-phobia' and finds 'commitment-light schemes that minimize risk exposure' to be 'increasingly common'.[7] These schemes aim to squeeze the poison out of the sting. Entering into a relationship is always a risky affair, since the thorns and traps of togetherness tend to reveal themselves gradually and their full inventory can hardly be composed in advance. Entering into relationships accompanied by a commitment to maintain them through thick and thin, whatever happens, is akin to signing a blank cheque. It portends the likelihood of confronting some as yet unknown and unimaginable discomforts and miseries with no escape clause to be invoked. The 'new and improved', 'commitment-light' relationships cut their anticipated duration down to the duration of the satisfaction they bring: commitment is valid until satisfaction fades or falls below an acceptable standard – and not a moment longer.

A few years ago, in the hope of stemming a rising tide still deemed to be only a transient fad, a battle was waged under the slogan 'A dog is for life, not just for Christmas' – it tried to prevent the abandonment of unwanted pets by January, when kids had become exhausted with the pleasure-giving potential of their Christmas gifts and had instead become weary of the daily chores demanded by the care of a pet. As we learn from Jeffries' study, however, this October a London branch is to be opened by a highly successful American firm, Flexpetz, that 'will enable customers to spend just a few hours or a few days' with one of their 'lovable and fully trained' dogs groomed for hiring. Flexpetz is one of the fast-multiplying companies specializing in 'services that offer traditional pleasures without the pain of ownership'. The trend to place transience where duration was once a rule is not confined to animal pets. At the far end of that trend there is a rapid rise in the number of households run by couples 'living together' but resentful of marriage vows. By 2005 the number of (presumably, not forever) cohabiting couples rose to well over 2 million.

There are at least two different ways to evaluate the impact of 'commitment-phobia' on the state and prospects of our contemporaries' happiness. One way is to welcome and applaud the lowering of the costs of pleasurable time. The spectre of future constraints that always hovered over committed partnerships was, after all, the proverbial fly able to blight and ruin a barrelful of the sweetest-smelling ointment; killing off that fly before it began its pernicious mischief is obviously no mean improvement. And yet, as Stuart Jeffries discovered, one of the largest car-hiring companies advises its customers to give personal names to the car they book time and again, on and off. Jeffries comments: 'the suggestion is poignant. It surely indicates that, even as we are less likely than ever before to commit to anything long term, the sentimental, perhaps even self-deluding pleasures of attachment remain with us – like ghosts of old ways of being.'

How true. Again and again, as so many times before, we find that one can't have a cake and eat it. Or that there are no free lunches. That there is a price to be paid for every gain. You gain freedom from the awkward task of caring daily for whatever you occasionally use: a car needs frequent washing, checking of tyres, changing of antifreeze and oil, renewing of the licence and insurance, and hundreds of other things, large and small, to be remembered and done, and you may fret and grumble about the bother and the waste of precious time that could be used for more pleasurable pastimes. But (surprisingly for some, expected for some others), attending to your car's needs is not an unambiguously unpleasant act. There is also a pleasure fully its own in the work having been done well and in you – precisely you, deploying your skills and proving your dedication – having done that work. And slowly, imperceptibly perhaps, that pleasure of pleasures is born: the 'pleasure of attachment', which owes its healthy growth in equal measure to the qualities of the object of your care and to the quality of your care. That elusive yet all-too-real and overwhelming pleasure of 'I–Thou', of 'we live for each other', 'we are one'. The pleasure of 'making a difference' that matters not only to you. Of making an impact and leaving a trace. Of feeling needed – and irreplaceable: a deeply pleasurable feeling, though so difficult to come by – and utterly unattainable, nay inconceivable, in the loneliness of self-concern and where attention is focused narrowly on self-creation, self-assertion and self-enhancement. That feeling may come only from a sediment of time, of time filled with your care – care being the precious yarn from which resplendent canvases of attachment and togetherness are woven.

Friedrich Nietzsche's ideal recipe for a fully human, happy life – an ideal gaining in popularity in our postmodern or 'liquid modern' times – is the image of 'Superman', the grandmaster of the art of self-assertion, able to evade or escape all and any of the fetters that trammel most ordinary mortals. 'Superman' is a true aristocrat – 'the powerful, the high-stationed, high-minded, who felt that they themselves were good, and that their actions were good',[8] until, that is, they surrendered to the backlash and blackmail of the vengeful *ressentiment* of 'all the low, the low-minded, the vulgar, the plebeian', retreated and lost their self-confidence and resolution. The 'Superman' (or, in another translation, the 'Higher Man') is, we can say, the aristocrat of the past (or, more precisely, the aristocrat as portrayed/imagined by Nietzsche to exist sometime in the past) resurrected or reincarnated in his pristine, unalloyed and uncut shape, shedding all the psychic leftovers of his interim misfortunes and humiliations, and recreating by his own will and action what to the original aristocrats of yore came naturally and matter-of-factly. ('The "well-born"', Nietzsche insisted, 'simply *felt* themselves the "happy"; they did not have to manufacture their happiness artificially . . . [or] to talk and lie themselves into happiness . . . Complete men as they were, exuberant with strength, and consequently *necessarily* energetic, they were too wise to dissociate happiness from action – activity becomes in their minds necessarily counted as happiness.'[9])

For Nietzsche's 'Higher Man', the power and resolve to disregard all rules and obligations is itself a supreme value which needs to be defended tooth and nail against compromise. A formidable obstacle on the road to Superman-style self-mastery, as he was soon to find out, was however the unyielding logic of time – in particular, according to the insightful commentary of Hanna Buczyńska-Garewicz,[10] the vexing yet indomitable 'staying power of the moment'. Self-mastery calls for the capacity to annul or at least neutralize the impact of external forces inimical to the self-creation project, yet the most formidable and overwhelming among such forces are precisely the traces, sediments, or leftovers of the prospective Superman's *own* drive to complete self-mastery; the consequences of the deeds he himself undertook and accomplished for its sake. The present moment (and every step on the way to complete self-mastery is one or another 'present moment') can't be neatly cut off from all that has already happened. A 'new beginning' is a fantasy that can't really be fulfilled, as the actor arrives at the current moment carrying indelible traces of all previous moments; and being a 'Superman', traces of past moments cannot but be the traces of his own past deeds. A fully self-sustained and self-contained 'episode' is a myth. Acts have consequences that outlive them. 'Will that designs the future is deprived of its freedom by the past,' comments Buczyńska-Garewicz. 'The will to settle old accounts diverts to the past, and this is [as Zarathustra, the literary spokesman for Nietzsche, put it] the teeth-gnashing and lonely torment of the will.' 'The staying power of the moment' is, we may say, the death knell of the trials of a 'new beginning'; to a trained ear, its sounding would be audible well before that 'new beginning' was attempted. In the gestation of self-mastery, the life of most embryos ends in miscarriage, if not abortion.

Nietzsche wants the 'Higher Man' to treat the past (including his own past deeds and commitments) with derision and feel unbound by them. But let me repeat: the past that slows down or arrests the flight of imagination and ties the hands of the designers of the future is nothing other than a sediment of past moments; present weaknesses are direct or oblique effects of their past displays of strength. And, horror of horrors, the more resourceful and resolute the aspiring 'Superhumans' (that is, men and women treating Nietzsche's call to arms seriously and resolving to follow it), the more deftly they master, manipulate and exploit each and any of the current moments to replenish and expand the happiness nesting in power and its displays, the deeper and yet more indelible the imprints of their 'accomplishments' are bound to be, and the narrower will be their future room for manoeuvre.

Nietzsche's 'Higher Man' seems to be doomed to end up as most of us, ordinary humans, do. Like, for instance, the hero of Douglas Kennedy's story of a 'man who wished to live his life'.[11] That man kept enclosing himself in the walls of obligations surrounding him, constantly thickened by ever more numerous traps and ambushes of family life, while all that time he dreamed of more freedom. He made resolutions to travel light, while adding to the burdens that kept him fixed to the ground, making the slightest movement a drudgery. Embroiled (or rather embroiling himself) in such irresolvable contradictions, Kennedy's hero did not suffer more oppression than the next person. He was no one's victim, not a target of anyone's resentment or malice. His dreams of the freedom to assert himself were foiled by no one except himself, and by nothing except his own efforts of self-assertion; the burden under which he sagged and groaned was made of the coveted and, indeed, cherished fruits of those efforts – of his career, his house, his kids, his ample credit – all those admirable and coveted 'goods of life' that offered a good reason, as Kennedy suggests, to get out of bed in the morning . . .

So whether this was or was not Nietzsche's intention, we may interpret his message (most probably against his intention . . .) as a warning: though self-assertion is human destiny, and though in order to implement that destiny a genuinely *super*human power of self-mastery would be needed, and though one would need to seek, summon and deploy a truly superhuman strength in order to fulfil that destiny and thereby to give justice to his own *human* potential – the 'Superman project' carries seeds of its defeat from the start. Perhaps unavoidably.

Our lives, whether we know it or not and whether we relish the news or bewail it, are works of art. To live our lives as the art of life demands, we must, just like the artists of any art, set ourselves challenges which are (at the moment of their setting, at any rate) difficult to confront point-blank; we must choose targets that are (at the moment of their choosing, at any rate) well beyond our reach, and standards of excellence that vexingly seem to stay stubbornly far above our ability (as already achieved, at any rate) to match whatever we do or may be doing. We need to *attempt the impossible*. And we can only hope, with no support from a trustworthy favourable prognosis (let alone from certainty), that with a long and grinding effort we may sometime manage to match those standards and reach those targets and so rise to the challenge.

Uncertainty is the natural habitat of human life – though the hope of escaping uncertainty is the engine of human life pursuits. Escaping uncertainty is a paramount ingredient, even if only tacitly presumed, of all and any composite images of happiness. This is why 'genuine, proper and complete' happiness always seems to reside some distance ahead: like a horizon, known to retreat whenever you try to come nearer.

1

Miseries of Happiness

The *Financial Times*, the obligatory daily reading for many thousands of the high and mighty, and many more also-rans who dream of joining them, publishes once a month a glossy supplement called *How to Spend It*. 'It' in the title means money. Or, rather, the cash left over after taking care of all the investments promising yet more cash, and paying the enormous house-and-garden and household bills, bespoke tailors' invoices, ex-partners' alimony dues, and debts for Bentley saloons. In other words, that margin of free choice (sometimes wide, and always wanted to be still wider) beyond the kinds of necessities to which the high and mighty are obliged to succumb. The 'it' to be spent is the hoped-for reward for days filled to the brim with nerve-wrackingly hazardous choices and many a sleepless night haunted by the horrors of false steps and wrong bets; 'it' is the joy which makes the pains worth suffering. In short, 'it' stands for *happiness*. Or, rather, for the hope of happiness that *is* happiness. Or at least is thought, and dearly hoped, to be . . .

Ann Rippin took the effort to browse through successive issues of *How to Spend It* to find out 'what a modern young man in the ascendant' is offered as the material source/token/evidence of happiness *achieved*.[1] Expectedly, all the suggested roads to happiness led through shops, restaurants, massage parlours and other sites where money can be spent. And big money indeed: £30,000 for a bottle of brandy, or a wine room at £75,000 to store it in the

company of other bottles and to enchant (make envious? humiliate? put to shame? devastate?) the company of friends invited to
visit and admire. But on the top of the prices that are sure to keep
almost the entire human race out of doors, some shops and restaurants have something extra to offer, something that will prevent
the rest of the race from showing up anywhere near the doors: a
secret address, excruciatingly difficult to obtain and bestowing
the very, very few who get it with the heavenly feeling of 'having
been chosen' – having been lifted to heights which ordinary
mortals could not dream of reaching. The kind of feeling perhaps
once experienced by mystics listening to the angelic messenger
announcing Divine grace, but in our sober, down-to-earth, matter-
of-factly 'happiness-now!' era seldom if ever available through
short cuts not passing by shops.

As one of the permanent contributors to *How to Spend It*
explains, what makes some exorbitantly costly perfumes 'so
beguiling' is the fact that they 'have been kept under wraps for
loyal clients'. In addition to an unusual fragrance, they offer an
olfactory emblem of magnificence and of belonging to the company
of the magnificent. As Ann Rippin suggests, that and similar kinds
of bliss combine belonging to an exclusive category – a company
barred to almost everyone else – with a badge of supreme taste,
discernment and connoisseurship (demonstrated by the sporting
of things or visiting of places not open to others). What that combination boils down to is knowledge of exclusivity: of being among
the selected few. The delights of the palate, of the eye, ear, nose
and fingers are multiplied by the knowledge that so few, if any,
are savoured by the palates and other organs of pleasurable sensation of anyone else – even if most people might give an arm and
a leg to taste them . . . Is it the sense of privilege that makes the
high and mighty happy? Is the progress towards happiness measured by a thinning out of the bevy of fellow travellers? Or is it
at least that belief, whether spelled out explicitly or kept under
cover and never articulated, that guides the pursuit of happiness
of *How to Spend It* readers?

Whatever the case may be, according to Rippin that way of
reaching the state of happiness is only half successful at best: the
momentary joys it brings dissolve and quickly vanish into long-
term anxiety. The 'fantasy world' spun by the editors of *How
to Spend It*, she insists, is marked by 'fragility and impermanence.

The struggle for legitimacy through magnificence and excess implies instability and vulnerability.' The occupants of that 'fantasy world' are aware that they 'can never have enough or, indeed, good enough to be safe. Consumption leads not to surety and satiety but to escalating anxiety. Enough can never be enough.' As one of the contributors to *How to Spend It* warns his readers, in a world in which 'everyone' can afford a luxury car, those who really aim high 'have no option but to go one better'.

This is what strikes you when (if) you take a closer look. But not everybody takes such a look, still fewer care to, and fewer still could if they cared – as the price of seats with good visibility is miles beyond their means and refuses to come any nearer. But the occasional glimpses of that sort of 'pursuit of happiness' which most of us can afford to see courtesy of the likes of *Hello* and other celebrity-courting magazines invite us to follow suit rather than warn us against trying. After all, this is what would make you one of those top people . . . The prospect of the pain of anxiety, however disconcerting, is a small price to pay for getting to the top. The message seems as sensible as it is straightforward: the way to happiness leads through the shops, and the more exclusive the shops, the greater the happiness reached. Reaching happiness means the acquisition of things other people have no chance or prospect of acquiring. Happiness needs *one-upmanship* . . .

High-street stores would not thrive were it not for the boutiques hidden in mews or with only selectively (and sparingly!) divulged addresses. Mews boutiques sell different products from high-street stores, but send the same message, promise to fulfil strikingly similar dreams. What the boutiques have done for the chosen few will surely lend authority and credibility to the promises of the mass copies on the high street. And the promises, in both cases, are strikingly alike: a promise makes you 'better *than* . . .' – and so able to overwhelm, humiliate, demean and diminish others who have dreamed of doing what you've done but failed. In short, the promise of the universal rule of one-upmanship working *for you* . . .

Another newspaper, known to be consulted by many *Financial Times* readers, regularly reviews novelties from the computer games market. Numerous computer games owe their popularity

to the fun they offer: *safe* and *freely* chosen rehearsals of that
practice of one-upmanship which in the real world is as *risky* and
dangerous as it is *obligatory* and unavoidable. These games allow
you to do what you have been nudged or might even have wished
to do, had you not been prevented because of your fear of getting
wounded, or your conscientious objections to wounding others.
One of these games, recommended as 'ultimate carnage' and a
'last man standing' 'demolition derby', is described by an enthu-
siastic-sounding and not particularly ironic reviewer:

> The most fun [. . .] are the events that demand you crash with the
> timing and precision to hurl your rag doll of a driver through the
> windscreen and high into the air in one of many arena events.
> From firing your hapless protagonist down enormous bowling
> alleys to skimming him like a smooth pebble across vast expanses
> of water, each is in equal measure ridiculous, violent and hilarious
> to play.

Your dexterity (your timing and precision in delivering blows)
against your protagonist's 'haplessness' (his inability to repay you
in kind) is what makes one-upmanship such fun and so 'hilarious
to play'. The self-esteem, the boost to the ego derived from the
display of your supreme skills, has been obtained at the expense
of the protagonist's humiliation. Your dexterity could be no less
and yet be only half as gratifying and half as much fun without
the protagonist in the rag-doll effigy, hurled through the wind-
screen while you stayed safely in the driver's seat.

Max Scheler noted as long ago as in 1912 that rather than
experiencing values before comparing them, the average person
appreciates a value only 'in the course of, and through comparison' with the possessions, condition, plight or quality of (an)other
person(s).[2] The snag is that a side-effect of such a comparison is
quite often the discovery of the non-possession of some appreciated value. That discovery and, yet more, the awareness that the
acquisition and enjoyment of that value is *beyond the person's
capacity*, arouse the strongest sentiments and trigger two mutually opposite, but equally vigorous reactions: an overwhelming
desire (all the more tormenting because of the suspicion that it
might be impossible to fulfil); and *ressentiment* – a rancour caused
by a desperate urge to ward off self-depreciation and self-

contempt by demeaning, deriding and degrading the value in question, together with its possessors. We may note that because it is composed of two mutually contradictory urges, the experience of humiliation begets a highly ambivalent attitude; a prototypical 'cognitive dissonance', a hotbed of irrational behaviour and an impenetrable fortress against arguments of reason. It is also a source of perpetual anxiety and spiritual discomfort for all those afflicted.

But those afflicted, as Max Scheler anticipated, add up to a great number of our contemporaries; the ailment is contagious and few if any denizens of the liquid modern society of consumers can boast of being fully immune to the threat of contamination. Our vulnerability, says Scheler, is unavoidable (and probably incurable) in a kind of society in which relative equality of political and other rights and formally acknowledged social equality go hand in hand with enormous differentiation of genuine power, possessions and education; a society in which everyone 'has the right' to consider himself equal to everybody else, while in fact being unable to equal them.[3]

In such a society, vulnerability is also (at least potentially) universal. Its universality, as well as the universality of the temptation of one-upmanship to which it is intimately related, reflects the inner unresolvable contradiction of a society that for *all* its members sets a standard of happiness which *most* of those 'all' are unable to match or are prevented from matching.

In advice which could have been addressed to the consumers of the society of consumers – since it was couched in a language they would easily understand and resorted to metaphors uniquely resonant with their worldview (even if not particularly in tune with their inclinations and preferences) – Epictetus, an ancient Roman slave self-transformed into a founder of the school of Stoic philosophy, suggested the following:

> Think of your life as if it were a banquet where you would behave graciously. When dishes are passed to you, extend your hand and help yourself to a moderate portion. If a dish should pass you by, enjoy what is already on your plate. Or if the dish hasn't been passed to you yet, patiently wait for your turn.
>
> Carry over the same attitude of polite restraint and gratitude to your children, spouse, career and finances. There is no need to

yearn, envy, and grab. You will get your rightful portion when it is your time.[4]

The trouble is, though, that our society of consumers does everything imaginable to make belief in the truth of Epictetus' reassuring *promise* appear contrary to experience and for that reason his *advice* of reticence, abstemiousness and caution is made difficult to accept. Our society of consumers also does everything imaginable to make the *practice* of Epictetus' advice a daunting task and uphill struggle. But it doesn't make it impossible. Society can (and does) render certain choices less likely to be made by humans than others. But no society could or can deprive humans of choice.

Is there something that can be said about happiness with confidence, without expecting opposition? There is: that happiness is a good thing – to be desired and cherished. Or that it is better to be happy than to be unhappy. But these two pleonasms are about *all* that can be said of happiness with well-grounded self-assurance. All other sentences involving the word 'happiness' are certain to arouse controversy. For an outside observer, one person's happiness may well be difficult to distinguish from another person's horror.

To say this is 'all' that could be said without risk of violent protests means, however, to say very little; most certainly, not much more than a dictionary-style definition of the word, which 'unpacks' its meaning by repeating what the word already implied, but using a few more words in the process. Contentious interpretations and standpoints start cropping up in profusion when it comes to *applying* that word to these rather than those things or states of things – and dictionary definitions will not stave off, stall or even mitigate the resulting controversies. It is not only *others* who may view with bewilderment or explicitly condemn or ridicule the decisions made by some people in applying the name to this rather than that situation; the decision-makers *themselves* are more likely than not to remain uncertain as to the propriety and/ or wisdom of their choice. Looking back, they may ask, puzzled, 'Is this what the whole hullabaloo was about? If this is the happiness I hoped for, has it been worth all that effort and all the sufferings apparently needed to reach it?!'

While Immanuel Kant struggled all his life (and to great effect) to sharpen and clarify foggy or moot concepts in the hope of arriving at a definition to 'settle the matter' in a way that was immune to all and any counter-argument and bound therefore to be acceptable and eventually accepted by all humans, he felt obliged to abandon such hope in the case of the 'happiness' concept. 'The concept of happiness', he declared, 'is such an indeterminate one that even though everyone wishes to attain happiness, yet he can never say definitely and consistently what it is that he really wishes and wills.'[5] We may add: when it comes to happiness one cannot be *both* definite *and* consistent. The more definite one is, the less is the chance of staying consistent. And little wonder, since being definite about the form which happiness must take means focusing attention and energy on the chosen model and leaving out, or casting into shadow, all the rest – whereas any model, when pursued at the expense of all the others, is bound to look ever more suspect as the graves of ever more stillborn, aborted or neglected possibilities multiply. Fulfilment is likely to arrive in a package deal with the temptation of inconsistency: of going back or moving sideways . . .

The desire for happiness, which, if we are to believe Plato, Socrates already proclaimed to be a brute fact of life, seems to be an eternal companion of human existence. But equally eternal seems to be the apparent impossibility of its complete, unquestionable, *je ne regrette rien* fulfilment and satisfaction. And equally eternal, notwithstanding all the frustrations this causes, is the impossibility of humans ever ceasing to desire happiness – and indeed trying their best to pursue it, attain it and retain it.

Following his usual strategy of resolving the issues arising from the complexity of the human predicament through decomposing them into an inventory of their simpler ingredients, Aristotle listed in his *Rhetoric* the personal qualities and achievements that – once possessed or gained – would gel into a happy life.[6] He agreed that happiness may be defined in a number of ways: as 'prosperity combined with virtue'; as 'independence of life'; as 'secure enjoyment of the maximum of pleasure'; as 'a good condition of property and body, together with the power of guarding one's property and body and making use of them'. But then he proceeded to offer a list of 'internal' and 'external' goods that are indispensable for happiness whichever formula of happy life may be chosen. The list, in his opinion, had empirical grounding, as it was composed of desires likely to be reported by all citizens of Athens: such as good birth, plenty of friends, good friends, wealth, good children, plenty of children, health, beauty, strength, large stature, athletic powers, fame, honour, good luck, virtue. No hierarchy of values in that list; all ingredients of happiness are placed at the same level of importance, suggesting that none can be sacrificed for another without happiness being impaired, and that the presence or abundance of any one could not truly compensate for the absence or dearth of another. That suggestion chimed well with the rest of Aristotle's life philosophy, famous for being suspicious of any radical, one-sided choices and instead advising moderation, balanced judgement and the choice of 'the golden mean' as the sole correct and effective strategy to be pursued amidst the notoriously variegated and inconsistent realities.

Contemporary readers are likely to be baffled, perhaps even put off, by the composition of Aristotle's list. Some of its items do not figure high among the qualities that contemporary men and women would mention if asked about their ideas of happiness; some other items would be viewed, to say the least, with mixed feelings. This is, however, a relatively minor irritant: what is likely to puzzle contemporary seekers of happiness the most is the tacit assumption that happiness is (could be, should be) a *state*, perhaps even a *steady* and *continuous* state, unchangeable once reached. Once all the items on the list are acquired and collected, and once it has been ensured they can be 'had' perpetually, they can be expected (so Aristotle implied) to provide happiness to their owners day in, day out – *in perpetuo*. This is precisely what our contemporaries would find most bizarre and unlikely to happen; they would, moreover, suspect such perpetual stability of having quite unprepossessing effects on the happiness of life in the unlikely event of it happening.

Most contemporary readers would surely consider it trivially obvious that to have more money is more propitious for happiness than having less, that having many good friends augurs better for happiness than having only a few or none, or that to be in good health is better than to be ill; but only a few readers, if any, will expect that the same things that make them happy on one day will go on entrancing them and giving them delight for ever and ever; and few will believe that a state of happiness can be attained once and for all, and that when attained it can last for the rest of life without needing more effort; that, in other words, happiness won't be spoiled if the pursuit of more and greater happiness grinds to a halt – despite the realization that 'from now on, nothing will change and everything will remain as it is'.

For most of our contemporaries, the prospect of 'more of the same' is not a value in its own right; it only becomes a value when it is complemented with a cancellation clause. 'More of the same' may be alluring at the moment of intense delight and exhilaration; but, as in other areas, most people will not expect the desire to last forever and would not wish the object of desire to remain 'the same' indefinitely. As Christopher Marlowe's Faust learned the hard way, wishing for a moment of bliss to stay 'the same' indefinitely is guaranteed to procure indefinite commitment to hell instead of indefinite happiness . . .

For most of our contemporaries it is rather the condition of 'being on one's way' (still some distance from the goal, pushed and pulled by as yet unsatisfied desires, compelled to dream – and to go on trying, and hoping, to make those dreams come true) that, despite being a testing time for patience and hard on the nerves, is to be welcomed as a value – and a most precious value to be sure. Most probably, our contemporaries would agree (at least in their hearts, if not in so many words) that the opposite of that condition, a state of rest, would not be a state of happiness, but of *boredom*; and for most of us 'being bored' is a synonym of extreme unhappiness, another name for the condition we fear most. If happiness can be a 'state', it can only be a state of excitement prodded by unfulfilment . . .

At the threshold of the modern era, 'the *state* of happiness' was replaced in the practice and dreams of happiness-seekers by the *pursuit* of happiness. Starting from that threshold, the greatest happiness has been and continues to be associated with the satisfaction derived from defying the odds and overcoming the obstacles, rather than with the rewards to be found at the far end of protracted defiance and long struggle. As Darrin McMahon, elaborating on the insights of Alexis de Tocqueville, observes in his remarkably comprehensive and perceptive study of the long story of happiness in 'Western' philosophy and culture,[7] just as the *longing* for equality in the America visited by de Tocqueville grew more insatiable with the growth in the equality *already gained*, so the unquenched desire and compulsive pursuit of happiness were (and still are) likely to absorb the happiness-seekers more rather than less as its material traces multiplied. In de Tocqueville's own words, 'happiness is a quality which ever retreats before them without getting out of sight, and as it retreats it beckons them on to pursue. Every instant they think they will catch it, and each time it slips through their fingers.'[8]

The advent of the pursuit of happiness as the prime engine of human thought and action augurs for some, though also portends for others, a veritable cultural, and also social and economic, revolution. *Culturally*, it presages, signals or accompanies the passage from perpetual routine to constant innovation, from the reproduction and retention of 'what has always been' or 'what was always had' to the creation and/or appropriation of what 'has never been' or 'what was never had'; from 'push' to 'pull', from need to desire, from cause to purpose. *Socially*, it coincides with the move from the rule of tradition to the 'melting of solids and profaning the sacred'. *Economically*, it triggers the shift from the satisfaction of needs to the production of desires. If the 'state of happiness' as a motive of thought and action was an essentially conservative and stabilizing factor, the 'pursuit of happiness' is a powerful destabilizing force; for the networks of interhuman bonds and their social settings, as well as for the human labours of self-identification, it is indeed a most effective antifreeze. It may well be considered the prime *psychological* factor in the causal complex responsible for the passage from the 'solid' to the 'liquid' phase of modernity.

On the psychological impact of the 'pursuit of happiness' promoted to the rank simultaneously of right, duty and the paramount purpose of life, de Tocqueville had the following to say:

> They [Americans] see it close enough to know its charms, but they do not get near enough to enjoy it, and they will be dead before they have fully relished its delights . . . [This] is the reason for the strange melancholy often haunting inhabitants of democracies in the midst of abundance, and for that disgust with life sometimes gripping them in calm and easy circumstances.[9]

Ancient sages guessed or anticipated that long before the dawn of the era of the 'universal pursuit of happiness'. They were keen to try to make sense of that apparent paradox – and to lay down a road avoiding or leading out of the trap it sets for the seekers of happiness. In his deliberations 'On the happy life' Lucius Anneus Seneca pointed out that

> The highest good is immortal, has no inclination to pass, it excludes surfeit as much as contrition. A noble mind never wavers in its resolutions, never becomes an object of self-contempt, never changes anything in its best way of life. It is the other way round with sensual pleasures: they cool down the moment they boil at their greatest heat. The volume of sensual pleasure is not great, and so it fills up rapidly, pleasure turns into surfeit and the original animation turns into dullness and sloth.[10]

For the sake of clarity, Seneca would have done better to reverse the reasoning recorded in the first sentence: rather than suggesting that good things are immortal, he might have said that it is things immortal that – precisely thanks to being immortal and resistant to the corroding impact of time – ought to be viewed as the highest good. Whatever persuasive power Seneca's counsel or warning might have had, it derived that power after all, from the ubiquitous and adamant human dream of ensnaring, disabling, slowing down and ultimately arresting the flow of time and depriving it of its eroding powers; from the unsatiated and insatiable yearning of mortal humans for the duration, infinite longevity, nay eternity of being. Having already tasted the fruit of the 'tree of knowledge', human mortals cannot and will not forget their mortality, however desperately and earnestly they might try; they are therefore unlikely ever to stop lusting after that other fruit, the fruit of the 'tree of life', the enchanted and enchanting fruit brutally and irrevocably denied them.

Until now, neither the distinction between 'worthy, since durable' and 'vain, since transient', nor the unbridgeable abyss separating the two, has disappeared for a moment from reflections on human happiness. Nonentity, the demeaning and humiliating insignificance of the individual bodily presence in the world by comparison with the unperturbed eternity of the world itself, has haunted philosophers (and non-philosophers, during their brief spells of falling into and staying in a philosophical mood) for more than two millennia. In the Middle Ages it was raised to the rank of the highest purpose and supreme concern of mortals, and deployed to promote spiritual values over the pleasures of the flesh – as well as to explain (and, hopefully, argue away) the pain and misery of the brief earthly existence as a necessary and therefore welcome prelude to the endless bliss of the afterlife. It returned with the advent of the modern era in a new garb: that of the futility of *individual* interests and concerns, shown to be abominably short-lived, fleeting and vagrant when juxtaposed with the interests of 'the *social* whole' – the nation, the state, the cause . . .

A powerful case for that refurbished, secularized response to individual mortality was constructed and extensively argued by Émile Durkheim, one of the founders of modern sociology. He strove to insert and settle 'society' in the place vacated by God and by Nature viewed as God's creation or embodiment – and thereby to claim for the nascent nation-state that right to articulate, pronounce and enforce moral commandments and command the supreme loyalties of its subjects; the right previously reserved for the Lord of the Universe and His anointed earthly lieutenants. Durkheim was fully aware of the purpose of his exercise: 'We must discover the rational substitutes for those religious motives that have, for so long, served as the vehicle for the most essential moral ideas.'[11] The true happiness Durkheim recommends be sought by humans has been redirected from a love of God and obedience to His Church to a love of nation and discipline to a nation-state. In both cases, though, the same argument is used of the superiority of eternity over transience.

> If our efforts result in nothing lasting, they are hollow, and why should we strive for that which is futile? . . . Of what value are our individual pleasures, which are so empty and short? . . .
>
> The individual submits to society and this submission is the condition of his liberation. For man freedom consists in deliverance from blind, unthinking physical forces; he achieves this by opposing against them the great and intelligent force of society, under whose protection he shelters. By putting himself under the

wing of society, he makes himself also, to a certain extent, dependent upon it. But this is a liberating dependence.[12]

In a reasoning that betrays quite a lot of family resemblance to Orwellian doublethink, an unconditional surrender to the stern demands of society and its appointed or self-appointed spokesmen – just like an obedience to God's commandments and their Church guardians it strove to replace – was re-presented as an act of *liberation*: liberation of the eternal from the grip of the transient, and of the spiritual from the prison of the flesh; in short, of true value from its fraudulent substitutes.

Seneca's cure, on the other hand, was concerned mostly with *self*-sufficiency and *self*-mastery. It was also thoroughly and resolutely *individualistic*. It relied neither on the omniscience of God nor on supreme reason and the omnipotence of society. It was addressed instead to 'noble minds', to the good sense, will and determination of individual human beings, and to the powers and resources those individuals individually commanded. It called on them to confront the miserable human condition each on their own; and to confront it point-blank – resisting and avoiding the ill-conceived and deceitful, sham therapy of averting their eyes from its sombre truth, as well as desisting from the chase after fleeting pleasures, a course that might allow them to forget that truth for as long as the chase continued, but not for a moment longer. This is probably what was meant by the verdict of Epicurus, which Seneca quotes with wholehearted approval: 'If you shape your life according to nature, you will never be poor; if according to people's opinions, you will never be rich';[13] or by his comment that 'there is nothing that brings greater trouble on us than the fact that we conform to rumour, thinking that what has won widespread approval is best, and that, as we have so many to follow as good, we live by the principle, not of reason, but of imitation'; and his warning that 'natural desires are limited; those which spring from false opinions have nowhere to stop, for falsity has no point of termination'; and, finally, by his own decision to pick out 'a mass crowd' as the thing 'particularly important to avoid', since 'the larger the size of the crowd we mingle with, the greater the danger'. 'Nothing is as ruinous to the character as sitting one's time at a show – for it is then, through the medium of entertainment, that vices creep into one with more than usual ease.'[14] In short: avoid the crowd, avoid mass audiences, keep your own counsel, which is the counsel of philosophy – of wisdom you can acquire and make your own. Man, says Seneca, is in his short sojourn on earth equal to God in His eternity. In one of his aspects, man is even superior to God: God has Nature to defend Him from fear – but whatever defence from fear man may attain, he has to, as he must, procure by his own wisdom.

The problem is, eternity is barred to humans, and so humans, all too painfully aware of that and entertaining little hope of appealing against that verdict of fate, seek to stifle and deafen their tragic wisdom in a hubbub of frail and fleeting pleasures. This admittedly being a false calculation – for the same reason which prompted it (that tragic wisdom can never be chased or conjured away for good) – they condemn themselves, whatever their material wealth, to perpetual spiritual poverty: to continuous unhappiness ('A man is as unhappy as he has convinced himself to be'[15]). Instead of seeking the way to happiness within the limits of their predicament, they take a long detour, hoping that somewhere along the route their odious and repulsive destiny may be escaped or fooled – only to land back in the despair that prompted them to start on their voyage of (dearly wished for, yet unattainable) discovery. The only discovery humans can possibly make on that voyage is that the route they have taken was but a detour that sooner or later will bring them back to the starting line.

> Whether we are caught in the grasp of an inexorable law of fate, whether it is God who as lord of the universe has ordered all things, or whether the affairs of mankind are tossed and buffeted haphazardly by chance, it is philosophy that has the duty of protecting us. She will encourage us to submit to God with cheerfulness and to fortune with defiance; she will show you how to follow God and hear what chance may send you.[16]

Vanity, vanity, all is vanity: Seneca seems to hammer that home, unknowingly repeating the message of his predecessor in Ecclesiastes: don't stoop to endowing the vainglorious with the attention, esteem and adoration it does not deserve. Seneca's successor in the long dynasty of Stoic philosophers, Marcus Aurelius, agrees, admonishing his readers, 'Your duty is to stand straight – not be held straight', and explaining:

> How all things quickly vanish, our bodies themselves lost in the physical world, the memories of them lost in time; the nature of all objects of the senses – especially of those that allure us with pleasure, frighten us with pain, or enjoy the applause of vanity – how cheap they are, how contemptible, shoddy, perishable, and dead . . .
>
> All things of the body stream away like a river, all things of the mind are dreams and delusions . . . What then can escort us on our way? One thing, one thing only: philosophy.[17]

Marcus Aurelius' advice is to keep one's distance from the hurly-burly, from all things that are contemptible because they are perishable and cheap, because they are shoddy: 'view earthly things as if looking down on them from some point high above.'[18] Doing that, you may resist and avoid the deceptive allure of things that will not, cannot, keep their promise of happiness, and you may resist the temptation to surrender that is bound to end in frustration.

> You know from experience that in all your wanderings you have nowhere found the good life – not in logic, not in wealth, not in glory, not in indulgence; nowhere. Where then is it to be found? In doing what man's nature requires . . . By having principles to govern his impulses and actions.[19]

And what should such principles be? Marcus Aurelius names some of them, selected so they can be displayed by all 'without any excuse of lack of talent or aptitude': integrity, dignity, hard work, self-denial, contentment, frugality, kindness, independence, simplicity, discretion, magnanimity. 'Remember that your directing mind becomes invincible when it withdraws into its own self-sufficiency . . . A mind free from passions is a fortress: people have no stronger place to retreat.'[20] Using the language of our times, we could say that Marcus Aurelius appoints personal character and conscience the ultimate refuge of happiness-seekers: the only place where dreams of happiness, doomed to die childless and intestate anywhere else, are not bound to be frustrated. The recipe for happiness offered by Marcus Aurelius is self-contained, self-referential and above all self-limiting. Know the false tracks, avoid them, accept the limits imposed by nature and from which it will not retreat. *Passions* – erratic as they are and knowing no bounds – would lead you astray, but fortunately you also have *mind*, a powerful weapon to disable passions and render them powerless. The secret of a happy life is to get a tight hold on your passions, while giving your mind free rein.

Many centuries later, Blaise Pascal seemed to have blended Seneca's and Marcus Aurelius' messages and distilled the shared essence from their compound:

> It is not in space that I must seek my human dignity, but in the ordering of my thought. It will do me no good to own land. Through space the universe grasps me and swallows me like a speck; through thought I grasp it.[21]

The trouble is, however, as Pascal hastened to add, that most people most of the time behave contrary to that sound advice. They seek happiness elsewhere, where it can't be found. 'The sole cause of human unhappiness', Pascal concluded in one of his most memorable phrases, 'is that he does not know how to stay quietly in his room.' Running out and around is just a way 'to take their minds off themselves'.[22] As there is little chance for thought when you are running, just keep running – and the excruciatingly taxing task of taking a closer look of yourself can be kept at arm's length: perpetually, infinitely, or at least as long as there is enough strength left in your legs to stay on the track. Most tracks, as we know, are closed circuits: round or elliptical, they lead nowhere; they are only meant to be run in circles. The name people choose for the game of what they believe to be the search for happiness (believe wrongly, to their own detriment, sentencing themselves to a bitter awakening) is *running*, not *arriving*.

> A given man lives his life free from boredom by gambling a small sum every day. Give him every morning the money he might win that day, but on condition that he does not gamble, and you will make him unhappy. It might be argued that what he wants is the entertainment of gaming and not the winning . . .

He must have excitement, he must delude himself into imagining that he would be happy to win what he would not want as a gift if it meant giving up gambling.[23]

Pascal suggests that people avoid looking inwards and keep running in the vain hope of escaping a face-to-face encounter with their predicament, which is to face up to their utter insignificance whenever they recall the infinity of the universe. And he censures them and castigates them for doing so. It is, he says, that morbid inclination to hassle around rather than stay put which ought to be blamed for all unhappiness.

One could, however, object that Pascal, even if only implicitly, does not present us with the choice between a happy and an unhappy life, but between two kinds of unhappiness: whether we choose to run or stay put, we are doomed to be unhappy. The only (putative and misleading!) advantage of being on the move (as long as we keep moving) is that we postpone for a while the moment of that truth. This is, many would agree, a genuine advantage of running *out of* rather than staying *in* our rooms – and most certainly it is a temptation difficult to resist. And they will choose to surrender to that temptation, allow themselves to be allured and seduced – if only because as long as they remain seduced they will manage to stave off the danger of discovering the *compulsion and addiction* that prompts them to run, screened by what is called '*freedom of choice*' or '*self-assertion*'. But, inevitably, they will end up longing for the virtues they once possessed but have now abandoned for the sake of getting rid of the agony which practising them, and taking responsibility for that practice, might have caused . . .

No wonder, therefore, that philosophers insist that it takes exclusive, sparsely awarded qualities like a 'noble mind', solid knowledge and strong character (sometimes also nerves of steel) to resist that temptation – and so refuse to surrender.

A few centuries after Pascal, in *Ordo Amoris*, Max Scheler insisted that the 'heart deserves to be called the core of man as a spiritual being much more than knowing and willing do'.[24] The 'heart' stands here for the choice between the sentiments of attraction and repulsion: love and hatred.

> The goods along the route of a man's life, the practical things,
> the resistances to willing and acting against which he sets his will,
> are from the very first always inspected and 'sighted', as it were,
> by the particular selective mechanism of his *ordo amoris*. . . . What
> he actually notices, what he observes or leaves unnoticed and
> unobserved, is determined by this attraction and this repulsion.

Man, says Scheler (and woman, as was self-evident to Scheler
but according to present-day politically correct usages requires an
explicit corroboration), before he (or she, passim) is an *ens cogi-
tans* or an *ens volens* (knowing or willing being), she or he is an
ens amans (loving being). 'Heart' lives solely by its own rules, the
rules that it sets in the course of its living, and is deaf or valiantly
disobedient to all other rules. In this egotism heart is similar to
Reason, also known to stubbornly decline all borrowing from
other logics. The heart, says Scheler with a bow to Pascal, 'has
its reasons' of which however Reason's 'understanding knows
nothing and can never know anything'[25] – since the heart's reasons
are not the 'objective determinations' and 'genuine necessities'
proclaimed by Reason as its home ground, and also its exclusive
and closely guarded domain, but 'self-styled' reasons, namely
motives and *wishes*. They are nothing like the reasons investigated
by Reason – even if they are 'no less rigorous, absolute and invio-
lable'. Arguments from reason are hapless and helpless when they
try to grasp the logic of the heart's itinerary, and even more impotent when they try to alter its course.

According to *its* reasons, the 'heart' constructs the world as a
world of *values*. And value, by its nature, is always *outstanding*,
always somewhat *ahead* of what is: nothing that is-already-here-
and-now can accommodate value in full. So there is no state of
affairs that already exists where a man or woman can be allowed
to sink into the cosy chair of self-satisfaction, to sit quietly or
stand still, once that state has been confronted by a heart stretching towards value ('Love loves and in loving always looks beyond
what it has in hand and possesses,' says Scheler.[26] The driving
impulse which arouses it may tire itself out; love itself does not
tire). Love, desire, lust set in action by a value are focused on
something that is-not-yet; their objects are all in the future, and
the future is an *absolute otherness*, inaccessible to the senses,
unavailable for scrutiny, evading all empirical tests and defying

all calculations. About objects with such qualities reason has nothing to say. It gladly throws in the towel when values enter the ring; it explains its retreat by declaring that all argument about preferences is out of its domain and therefore below its dignity: *de gustibus non est disputandum* – one does not dispute matters of taste. It admits that its toolbox is empty by acknowledging that values can neither be derived from, nor confirmed or refuted by, 'the facts of the matter'. Values are left alone in the ring. No opposition in sight, yet no support either. It is all up to them now. And so love is indeed in no danger of being tired out. It is also, however, devoid of the hope of resting. It stumbles from one gambit to another, never sure of what the endgame will be and forever uncertain how fortuitous or fatal the opening will prove to have been.

'When we survey a man's whole life or a long sequence of years and events,' Scheler observes, 'we may indeed feel that each single event is completely accidental, yet their connection, however unforeseeable every part of the whole was before it transpired, reflects exactly that which we must consider the core of the person concerned.'[27] The message is clear enough: it all boils down to a person's character, something we all know we have but, however long we live, can never be sure what it is like (we are surely deluded if we presume that we are . . .). An individual's *destiny* is *not* his or her *fate*. What we, in imitation of the infamous gesture of Pontius Pilate, call 'fate' in order to disown it as 'not of our doing', is shaped in fact in the course of our life; of the individual life in great measure, but wholly in the life of the species. Knowingly or not, you and I and all of us shape our destinies singly, severally or all together, and only once we've run out of the resources and/or of the will needed to go on with the job of shaping and reshaping, it does turn into 'fate'.

To cut a long story short, we tend to lay our personal destiny at the doorstep of impersonal fate not because our choices have no impact on the itinerary of our lives; we do it because at the moment we are making that impact we are unaware (and can't be *fully* aware) of what sort of impact we have made or are about to make. In other words, we make *a* difference, though we can't be sure *what* difference we make. Whatever we do or desist from doing *will make* a difference – this we can't help. But we can only wish and try to *know* in advance what sort of difference we are likely to make. We do try – though not necessarily as hard as we could. What stops us from trying harder?

One of the factors that makes trying harder is the nature of *ordo amoris* itself: for the happiness it offers, it sets a price. The price it sets is often a compromise, but sometimes it is also an unreciprocated, unilateral self-sacrifice; in Erich Fromm's succinct expression, 'love is primarily giving, not receiving'.[28] Either kind of price may brandish the prospect of limiting the extent and the intensity of happiness – a vision not everyone, at every time, will accept gladly. If love is by its very nature a tendency to join the objects of love (a person, a company of persons, a cause) in their struggle towards fulfilment, to assist them in that fight, to promote that struggle and bless the fighters, then 'to love' means to be ready to abandon self-concern for the sake of its object, to render one's own happiness a reflection, a side-effect of that object's happiness – by the same token (to repeat after Lucan, two millennia later), giving 'hostages to fate'. By loving we try to recast fate into destiny; but by following the demands of love, the logic of *ordo amoris*, we make our destiny a hostage to that fate. The two tendencies, apparently in discord, are in fact Siamese twins and can't be separated.

This is why love tends nowadays to be simultaneously desired and feared. This is also why the idea of commitment (to another person, to a company of persons, to a cause), and particularly of unconditional and indefinite commitment, has fallen out of popular favour. To the detriment of those who let it lapse – since love, and self-abandonment and commitment to the Other, which is what love consists of, create the only space where the intricate dialectics of destiny and fate can be seriously confronted.

But with the formula of happiness that elevates 'one-upmanship' to the rank of guiding principle, with individuals overwhelmed by a 'thirst for excitement and diminishing willingness to fit with others, to subordinate themselves or do without', 'how can two individuals who want to be or become equals and free discover the common ground on which their love can grow?', ask Ulrich Beck and Elisabeth Beck-Gernsheim; 'How can the other person avoid becoming an additional hindrance, if not a disruptive factor?'[29] These question sound rhetorical, loaded as they are in advance with straightforward answers and foregone conclusions. 'One-upmanship' – in the authors' version, 'I am what matters: I, and

You as my assistant, and if not You then some other You'[30] – can't easily be squared with partnership and love, and particularly a longed-for love which is hoped to be a bulwark against the spectre of loneliness and a breakwater guarding a haven of tranquillity from the storm of the open seas. 'In the post-romantic world', as Ehrenreich and English point out,

> where the old ties no longer bind, all that matters is *you*: you can be what you *want* to be; you *choose* your life, your environment, even your appearance and your emotions . . . The old hierarchies of protection and dependency no longer exist, there are only free contracts, freely terminated. The marketplace, which long ago expanded to include the relations of production, has now expanded to include *all* relationships.[31]

'Sacrificial culture is dead,' declared Gilles Lipovetsky bluntly in his 1993 postface to his stage-setting 1983 study of contemporary individualism. 'We've stopped recognizing ourselves in any obligation to live for the sake of something other than ourselves.'[32]

Not that we have turned deaf to our concerns with the misfortunes of other people, or with the sorry state of the planet; nor have we ceased to be outspoken about such worries. Neither is it the case that we've stopped declaring our willingness to act in defence of the downtrodden, as well as in protection of the planet they share with us; nor that we have stopped acting (at least occasionally) on such declarations. The opposite seems to be the case: the spectacular rise of egotistic self-referentiality runs paradoxically shoulder to shoulder with a rising sensitivity to human misery, an abhorrence of violence, pain and suffering visited on even the most distant strangers, and regular explosions of focused (remedial) charity. But, as Lipovetsky rightly observes, such moral impulses and outbursts of magnanimity are instances of 'painless morality', morality stripped of obligations and executive sanctions, 'adapted to the Ego-priority'. When it comes to acting 'for the sake of something other than oneself', the passions, well-being and physical health of the Ego tend to be both the preliminary and the ultimate considerations; they also tend to set the limits to which we are prepared to go in our readiness to help.

As a rule, manifestations of devotion to that 'something (or someone) other than oneself', however sincere, ardent and intense, stop short of self-sacrifice. For instance, the dedication to green causes seldom if ever goes as far as adopting an ascetic lifestyle, or even a partial self-denial. Indeed, far from being ready to renounce a lifestyle of consumerist indulgence, we will often be reluctant to accept even a minor personal inconvenience; the driving force of our indignation tends to be the desire for a superior, safer and more secure consumption. In Lipovetsky's summary, 'disciplinary and militant, heroic and moralizing individualism' has given way to 'individualism à la carte', 'hedonist and psychological', one that 'makes of the intimate accomplishments the principal purpose of existence'.[33] We don't seem to feel any longer that we have a task or a mission to perform on the planet, and there is apparently no legacy left which we feel obliged to preserve, having been appointed its wardens.

Concern with the way *the world* is managed has given way to concern with *self*-management. It is not the state of the world, complete with its inhabitants, that tends to worry us and cause us concern, but what is in fact an end-product of recycling its outrages, inanities and injustices into spiritual discomforts and emotional giddiness that impair the psychological balance and peace of mind of the concerned individual. This may be, as Christopher Lasch was one of the first to note and articulate, the result of transforming 'collective grievances into personal problems amenable to therapeutic intervention'.[34] 'The new narcissists', as Lasch memorably called the 'psychological men' able to perceive, scrutinize and assess the state of the world solely through the prism of personal problems, are 'haunted not by guilt but by anxiety'. In recording their 'inner' experiences, they 'seek not to provide an objective account of a representative piece of reality but to seduce others' into giving them 'their attention, acclaim or sympathy' and thus to shore up their faltering sense of self. Personal life has become as warlike and as full of stress as the marketplace itself. The cocktail party 'reduces sociability to social combat'.[35]

With nothing much on which to rest that craved-for security of one's social standing, rebounding as self-confidence and self-esteem, except the personal assets personally owned or personally to be acquired, no wonder that demands for recognition, as Jean-Claude Kaufmann puts it, 'overflow society'. 'Everyone watches intently for approbation, admiration or love in the eyes of others.'[36]

And let's note that the grounds for self-esteem provided by the 'approbation and admiration' of others are notoriously feeble. Eyes are known to shift, and the things on which they fall or over which they skate are notorious for their propensity to twist and turn in ways impossible to predict, so the propulsion and compulsion to 'watch intently' never really grinds to a halt. The tepidity of today's vigilance may well turn yesterday's approval and acclaim into tomorrow's condemnation and derision. Recognition is like the cardboard rabbit in a sweepstake chase: forever chased by dogs, never locked in their jaws.

Notoriously, the future eludes description and defies prognostication. But neither does the past supply the kind of orientation it is much too often – though misleadingly, deceitfully – credited with offering. The 'legacy' of the past is only a raw material intended for the recycling plants of the future. As Hannah Arendt pointed out, there is no testament to specify what belongs to whom; what we call 'legacy' or 'heritage' is little more than the act of surrendering the past to the mercy of fate.[37] The past is hostage to the future – and bound to remain a hostage forever, however often its liberation or manumission has been zealously negotiated, and however high the ransom already paid. Orwell's famed dictum, 'who controls the past controls the future; who controls the present controls the past', stays topical and all too credible long after its original inspiration – the ambitions and practices of the totalitarian 'Ministries of Truth' – sank into the past (and for many of our contemporaries into oblivion). The snag, however, is that few if any individuals can now credibly boast that they control the present, while fewer still can be credited with really doing what they brag they can do.

With the present cut off on both sides – from the past, now denied the authority of an accredited guide, and from a future that already ignores the commands and immolations of the present and treats them with a negligence not unlike that with which the present treats its past, the world appears to remain perpetually *in statu nascendi* – in a 'state of becoming'. The course that becoming will eventually take is chronically underdetermined; its direction tends to shift (or drift) at random rather than to obey any specific – cryptic but still guessable – order of the sort postulated not too long ago under the name of the 'laws of history'.

The philosopher Martin Heidegger suggested that we notice
things, become conscious and aware of them, draw them into the
focus of our attention and make them into targets of intentional
action only once there is 'something wrong' – when they go bust,
start behaving in an odd way we haven't been used to, or otherwise 'fall out of the norm', thereby challenging our tacit presump-
tions about what the world is like and what can be expected to
happen in it.

We could say, with Heidegger, that the mother of knowledge and simultaneously the spur to action is *disappointment*.
Historian Barrington Moore Jr pointed out that in the past people
tended to rebel and take up arms not so much to win 'justice' as
to defeat 'injustice'. 'Injustice' was the event that disturbed a life
that was so regular and routine as to stay virtually unnoticeable,
causing no sensation of harm being done and no feeling of pain
(let alone an 'unjust' pain); they could only visualize 'justice' (if
this is what they called the purpose of their rebellion) as an act
of denial, rejection, cancelling, balancing out or repairing that
'injustice'. More often than not, the demand for justice was a
conservative call, harking back to something lost or thought to
have been lost; a drive to restore what had been forcefully
('unjustly', 'undeservedly') taken away, and to go back to enjoying
(dreadful, but familiar and used to, 'normal') old times.

To put it in a nutshell, the familiarity of the setting did not
necessarily make people happy, but it set the standard of the
normal or 'natural', and therefore 'unchallengeable' and 'unavoidable'. It was the *un*familiar departure from the standard and the
norm, a novelty by definition 'unnatural' and so given to manipulation, that tended to be felt as an outrage: and so to shock, cause
an outcry and prompt people to take up arms. Once the unfamil-
iar broke in, the familiar turned (if only retrospectively) into the
embodiment of happiness: once under assault, the familiar felt
like happiness itself. The feudal serfs, for instance, would hardly
ever have considered themselves happy when they worked the
lord's fields six days a week: but adding an hour more to the lord's
customary demands would make them 'realize' how happy they
must have been when their villein duties took only six days a week
and not an hour more. The outrage of the happiness *denied* might
then prompt them to rebel. In more recent times, it has been
widely noted that even the sharpest inequality of wages customar-

ily 'due' to different categories of hired hands have been on the whole accepted placidly by those at the lower levels of the scale; it was when they fell *behind* people who had thus far been treated as their *equals* that they felt 'deprived' – denied their rights, including the right to happiness – and were prompted to rebel and strike. 'Deprivation', experienced as an injustice having been done and crying out to be remedied for the sake of happiness, has been as a rule of a *relative* variety.

Now, as much as then, deprivation means unhappiness. Added to the material hardships it may bring are the degradation and humiliation of finding oneself at the receiving end of deprivation, a hard blow to self-esteem and a menace to social recognition. Now, as then, deprivation is always 'relative'; to feel deprived, a benchmark is needed against which to measure one's own condition. A person may feel deprived and for that reason unhappy because they have fallen below the standard they enjoyed in the past, or because they are falling behind their equals of yesterday who now, suddenly, are surging ahead. Thus far, there is nothing new under the sun. What is new is the status of the benchmark(s) that may produce the experience of 'having been deprived' and thus inject an added urgency and vigour into the pursuit of happiness.

The rules discovered by Heidegger or Barrington Moore Jr relied on a world in which the line separating the 'normal' from the 'abnormal' could be neatly drawn; in which 'normal' was a synonym of what was most common, monotonous, repetitive, routine and resistant to change. Those rules were at home in a world in which things were explicitly expected to last or tacitly assumed to persist in the same place and condition and retain the same shape unless they were thrown out of their inertia by a force that was extra-ordinary (that is, 'out of order' and so by definition unpredictable) and as a rule external. Duration and sameness were the guiding principles of such a world. Any change was incremental and slow enough to be imperceptible: cast among durable things, people had abundant time to 'adjust', 'accommodate', and slowly and for that reason imperceptibly adopt new habits, routines and expectations. Without difficulty and hesitation, they could tell the 'regular' from the 'accidental', and the 'legitimate' from the 'unwarranted'. However atrocious or miserable their condition might 'objectively' appear, they might not feel uncomfortable so long as they knew their place and choices and were aware of what was in store and how to respond to what was likely to come. The sole meaning the idea of 'happiness' might have had for them was the absence of unhappiness; and 'unhappiness' was most likely to mean a disruption of routine and frustration of expectation.

Inside the tightly stratified societies marked by a sharp polarization of access to both material and symbolic values (prestige, respect, insurance against humiliation), it is the people situated 'in the middle', in the space stretching between the top and the bottom, who tend to be most sensitive to the threat of unhappiness. Whereas the upper classes *needed* do little or nothing at all to *retain* their superior condition, and the bottom classes *could* do little or nothing at all to *improve* on their inferior lot, for the middle classes everything they didn't have but coveted appeared to be for the taking, while everything they had and cherished could be easily – in a single moment of inattention – be lost. More than any other category of people, they were bound to live in a state of perpetual anxiety, constantly oscillating between the fear of unhappiness and brief intervals of apparent safety and its enjoyment. The offspring of middle-class families would need to strive hard and lean over backwards if they wished to keep the family fortune intact and to re-create, by their own zeal and acumen, the comfortable social standing their parents enjoyed: it was mostly to narrate the risks and fears typically related to such a task that terms like 'fall', 'social degradation', or the agony and humiliation of being déclassé, were coined. Indeed, the middle class was the only class of the class-divided society that remained permanently squeezed between two sociocultural borders, each of those borders being reminiscent of a front line rather than of a safe and peaceful frontier. The upper border was a site of incessant reconnaissance sorties and feverish defence of its few bridgeheads; the lower border had to be closely watched – it could easily let intruders in, while offering little protection to insiders unless they kept it tightly sealed and intensely guarded.

Among the reasons to interpret the advent of the modern era as a transformation promoted mostly by middle-class interests (or, following Karl Marx, as a victorious 'bourgeois revolution'), the typically middle-class obsessions with the frailty and untrustworthiness of social standing, and the equally obsessive efforts at defence and stabilization loom very large indeed. When they sketched the contours of a society knowing no unhappiness, the utopian blueprints proliferating at the dawn of the modern era reflected, recycled and recorded predominantly *middle-class* dreams and longings; the society they portrayed was as a rule purified of *uncertainties* – and above all of the ambiguities and insecurities of *social position*, the rights it bestowed and the duties it demanded. However much the blueprints might have differed, they were unanimous in choosing duration, solidity and the absence of change as the essential premises of human happiness. Inside the utopian cities (virtually all utopias were urban), positions were many and different – but every resident was safe and secure in the position allocated to him. More than anything else, utopian blueprints visualized the end to uncertainty and insecurity: to wit, a fully predictable social setting free of surprises and calling for no further reforms and reshuffles. The 'good' or even the 'perfectly good' society divined in utopias was a society that was to put paid once and for all to all the most typically middle-class anxieties.

One may say that the middle classes were an avant-garde, experiencing and exploring, before the rest of society, the principal contradiction of the existential condition destined to become a well-nigh universal characteristic of modern life: the perpetual tension between two values, security and freedom, equally coveted and indispensable for a happy life – but frightfully difficult, alas, to reconcile and be enjoyed together. Because of its precarious position, and its need to treat as a forever unfinished task what the other parts of society could view as a (welcome or unsolicited) 'free gift' of fate which they needed do little to retain and could do little to change, middle class was particularly predisposed to face and confront that tension. This circumstance may explain in part why the way the challenges and concerns originally specific to the middle classes spread to the bulk of modern societies has been widely recorded, rightly though not necessarily for the right reasons, as 'embourgeoisement'. There were also, however, other reasons than strictly class-related ones why the rest of the society followed suit after the middle classes.

In his recent, incisive study of the birth, development, internal contradictions and unanticipated consequences of the modern

concepts of the good society and the good life, Jean-Claude
Michéa traces the origins of the 'modern project' to the 'fear of
violent death, of mistrusted neighbours, of ideological fanaticism'
and to the desire for 'a life at last tranquil and pacified'[38] – both
being reactions to the convulsions and agonies of the frightful
invention of early modern times: ideological civil wars in the form
of the 'religious wars' of the sixteenth to seventeenth centuries. In
the words of Leopold von Ranke, historian of that blood-soaked
era in European history, 'before the fanatical conception of reli-
gion, the morality which lies at the foundation of all civilization
and of all human society vanished . . . The minds of men were
filled with wild fantasies, which made them afraid of themselves,
and caused the very elements to appear fraught with terror.'[39] 'The
wild mountains resounded with the shrieks of the murdered, and
were fearfully lighted up by the fire of their solitary dwellings.'[40]
In a recent comment by Richard Drake, 'reciprocal slaughters and
assassinations, of the kind seen today between Sunnis and Shiites
in Iraq'[41] (and we may add: seen only yesterday between Serbs,
Croats and Bosnian and Kosovo Muslims), a seemingly endless
cycle of murderous retaliations, engulfed France, and most of
Western Europe, in blood. The horror of incessant wars that set
brother against brother and neighbour against neighbour and
stripped them all of the last shred of mutual loyalty, pity and
compassion inspired Blaise Pascal to name war as 'the greatest of
evils' and Hobbes to select the 'war of all against all' as the most
prominent characteristic of the natural state of humankind.

Like the Angel of History painted by Paul Klee and famously
reflected upon by Walter Benjamin, contemporaries fixed their
horrified eyes on past and present atrocities and abominations;
repelled by what they saw – the seas of blood and oceans of
human misery – they *retreated* into the future. They were *pushed*
rather than *pulled*; it was not a vision of bliss that drew them *into
the future*; it was rather the sight of agony and wretchedness that
propelled them *away from the past*. With their eyes fixed on the
past, they could neither see nor have time to imagine that future
into which they were pushed – let alone to describe it in any detail.
What they wished was not a *perfect* world, Michéa suggests, but
a world of a *lesser evil*. They would be ready to forgive all sorts
of shortcomings and minor lapses with which that other world
might yet prove to be (who knew?) burdened, if only humanity
were drawn out from the mire of mutual hatred, suspicion and

treachery in which it had been plunged by the centuries-long hostilities born of ideological passions.

Having found no lifeboat huge and shipshape enough to accommodate the whole of humanity, they settled for individual life-jackets: self-interest, that sharp-eyed faculty owned by every human being, a faculty temporarily suffocated by blind passion, its arch-enemy, but certain to be resuscitated, to recuperate and come into its own once liberated from the collective madness. 'How to escape that war of all against all, if virtue is but a mask of self-pride, if one can trust no one and can count solely on oneself?': so Jean-Claude Michéa reconstructs the mystery that haunted Pascal's and Hobbes's contemporaries.[42] Individual *self-interest* was the solution they believed they had found for that mystery. 'Interest will not lie', as Marchamont Nedham, inspired by the Duke de Rohan, declared in a book published in 1659.[43] Escape from the horror of war, cruelty and violence leads through the revival and liberation of egoism, the natural endowment to which all and every human individual may and most certainly will resort, given the chance. Allow humans to follow that natural inclination, to be concerned with their own well-being, comfort and pleasure, combining in the state of happiness – and they will surely soon find out that murder, cruelty, plunder and theft can hardly serve their self-interest. As Immanuel Kant was to sum up the point in his formula of 'categorical imperative': reason will tell them that to serve their interest properly they should do to others as they would wish the others to do to them, and refrain from doing what they would loathe to be done to them; that is, they should respect other people's interests and resist all temptations to be cruel and threatening to others and their property.

More often than not, hopes are difficult to recognize in the realities they sediment. The 'invisible hand' of the market operated by selfish individuals in search of their own wealth and pleasure seemed to be rather reluctant or impotent to save humans from the horrors of reciprocal cruelties; most certainly, it managed neither to liberate most humans from the bondage of passions, nor to make completely happy those few whom it succeeded in freeing. Somehow, passions – impulses allegedly inimical to self-interest and bound to be resented and perhaps stifled following a sober and rational calculation of personal gain – proved to be every bit as indispensable to happiness as was the pursuit of purely personal advantage. It transpired that in order to draw satisfaction from their life, humans need to give and to love and to share as much as they need to take, to defend their privacy and to guard their own. To the abstruse, contradiction-fraught quandary commonly known under the name of the human condition, there seem to be no simple, straightforward, single-issue solutions.

Jean-Jacques Rousseau suggested that humans need to be *coerced* into *freedom*; at least into the freedom adumbrated by philosophers and regarded by them as an implacable demand of reason. We may say that the world spawned by the 'modern project' behaves, in practice if not in theory, as if humans had to be coerced into pursuing *happiness* (at least the happiness adumbrated by their self-appointed advisers and hired counsellors, as well as the writers of advertising copy) . . . Twenty-four hours a day and seven days a week humans tend to be drilled, groomed, exhorted, cajoled and tempted to abandon the ways they have considered right and proper, to turn their backs on what they have held dear and what they thought had been making them happy, and to become different from what they are. They are pressed to turn into workers ready to sacrifice the rest of their lives for the sake of competitive enterprise or enterprising competition, into consumers moved by infinitely expandable desires and wants, into citizens embracing fully and unreservedly the 'there is no alternative' edition of the 'political correctness' of the day, which prods them, among other things, to be closed and blind to disinterested generosity and indifferent to the common weal in case it can't be deployed to enhance their egos . . .

As historical evidence has abundantly shown, the *coercion to be free* seldom, if ever, leads to freedom. I leave it to readers to decide whether the *coercion to seek happiness*, in the form practised in our liquid modern society of consumers, makes the coerced happy. Finding an answer to that question through putting it to the test of practice has been, as a matter of fact, left to us as individual men and women. Our lives have been set as an inconclusive series of experiments hoped to definitely prove or disprove the validity of the proposition. Artists are adventurous, experimenting creatures; and all of us, men and women, old and young, having been told that life is an object of art, given/left to individual artists to shape, are nudged and seduced to take up the risks that such art inevitably entails.

2

We, the Artists of Life

A most acute and insightful observer and analyst of intergenerational change, and particularly of emergent styles of life, Hanna Swida-Ziemba, noted that 'people of past generations situated themselves in the past as much as in the future'; for the new, contemporary young, however, only the present exists. 'The young people to whom I talked during the research conducted in 1991–3 asked: Why there is so much aggression in the world? Is it possible to achieve full happiness? Such questions are no longer important to them.'[1]

Swida-Ziemba spoke of Polish youth. But in our fast-globalizing world she would have found very similar trends wherever she focused her inquiry. The data collected in Poland, a country just emerging from long years of an authoritarian rule which artificially conserved modes of life left behind elsewhere, and which strictly regimented the manner in which happiness was permitted to be pursued, only condensed and telescoped worldwide trends, making them more acute, and therefore more salient and easier to note.

What probably prompts you to ask 'where does aggression come from?' is the urge to do something about it; it is because you feel strongly about it and earnestly wish to stem aggression or fight back against it, that you desire to learn where the roots of aggression lie. Presumably, you are keen to reach those places where aggressive impulses or aggressive schemes breed and are exuberant – and then to try to incapacitate and destroy them. And if this guess about your motives is correct, you must resent a world infused with aggressiveness as uncomfortable or downright unfit for human life, and for that reason iniquitous, but you must also believe that such a world *could* be remade into another, more peaceful one, hospitable and friendly to humans – and believe as well that if you try, as try you should, *you* might become part of the force able and bound to make it into such a world. Whereas when you ask whether full happiness can be attained, you probably believe in achieving, singly or severally, a more agreeable, worthy and satisfying way of living your life – and are willing to undertake the kind of effort, perhaps even bear the kind of sacrifice called for by any worthy cause, and the uneasy tasks it sets its followers. In other words, by asking that question you've implied that rather than accepting the extant state of affairs placidly and meekly, you are inclined to measure your strength and ability by the standards, tasks and goals you've set yourself for your life – and not the other way round: measuring your ambitions and goals by the strength you think you have been given or can muster at the moment.

Surely, you must have made, and followed, such assumptions; otherwise you wouldn't have been bothered to ask such questions. For these questions to occur to you, you must first believe that the world around you is not 'given' once and for all, that it can be changed, and that you yourself can be changed through applying yourself to the job of changing it. You must have assumed that the state of the world can be different than it is now, and that how different it may become depends no less (if not more) on what you do, than what you do or desist from doing depends on the state of the world – past, present and future. You must have trusted your own ability to *make a difference*: a difference in the course of your own life, but also in the world in which that life is lived. To cut a long story short: you must have believed that you are an *artist* able to create and shape things as much as you yourself might be a *product* of that creation and shaping . . .

The proposition 'life is a work of art' is not a postulate or an admonition (of the 'try to make your life beautiful, harmonious, sensible and full of meaning – just as painters try to make their paintings, or musicians their compositions' kind), but a statement of fact. Life can't *not be* a work of art if this is a *human* life – the life of a being endowed with will and freedom of choice. Will and choice leave their imprint on the shape of life, in spite of all and any attempts to deny their presence and/or to hide their power by ascribing the causal role to the overwhelming pressure of external forces that impose 'I must' where 'I will' should have been, and so narrow the scale of plausible choices.

Being an individual (that is, being responsible for your choice of life, your choice among choices, and the consequences of the choices you chose) is not itself a *matter of choice*, but a *decree of fate*. All too often, however, one needs to exercise that responsibility under conditions that entirely elude one's own, intellectual as well as practical, grasp. Human life consists of a perpetual confrontation between 'external conditions' (perceived as 'reality', by definition a matter always resistant to, and all too often defying, the agent's will) and the designs of its 'auctors' (authors/actors): their aim to overcome the active or passive resistance, defiance and/or inertia of matter and to remould reality in accordance with their chosen vision of the 'good life'. Of that vision, Paul Ricoeur says that it is 'a haze of ideals and dreams of achievement', in the dim light of which the degree of life's success or failure is traced and ascertained.[2] In that light certain steps and their results, though not others, are judged as sensible, and certain purposes, but not others, are set aside as not merely instrumental, but 'auto-telic': that is, as objectives 'good in their own right', with no need of being justified and vindicated as means to the implementation of some other, higher objective.

Visions of the good life are compared by Ricoeur to a nebula. Nebulae are full of stars, you won't be able to count them all, and countless shining and blinking stars charm and tempt. Between them, the stars might mitigate the darkness enough to allow the wanderers to trace a path in the wilderness – some sort of path; but which star should orient one's steps? And at what point should one decide whether selecting this star for a guide from among the multitude has been a felicitous or an unlucky decision? When should one conclude that the chosen path leads nowhere, and that the time has arrived to abandon it, turn back and make another, hopefully better choice? Notwithstanding the discomforts already brought by walking the previously selected road, such a resolution may be an unwise step: abandoning a hitherto followed star may prove to be an even graver and in the end more regrettable error, and you may find that the alternative path leads to even greater hardships; you don't know, nor are you likely to know all that for sure. Heads or tails, your chances of winning or losing look even.

There is no straightforward, unambiguous remedy for all such quandaries. However hard one tries to the contrary, life is lived in the company of uncertainty. Each decision is bound to remain arbitrary; none will be free of risks and insured against failure and belated regrets. For every argument in favour of a choice, a counter-argument, no less weighty, can be found. However bright might be the light of the nebula, it will not insure us against the eventuality of being forced, or desiring, to turn back to the starting point. Embarking on our way to a decent, dignified, satisfying, worthy (and, yes, happy!) life, we try to prevent errors and escape uncertainty by trusting in a star, chosen for its reassuring brightness, to guide us. All that, however, only soon to find out that our choice of guiding star was in the last account *our* choice, pregnant with risks as all our choices have been and are bound to be – and *our* choice, made on *our* responsibility, it will remain to the end . . .

As Michel Foucault suggested, only one conclusion follows from the proposition that 'identity is not given': our identities (that is, the answers to questions like 'Who am I?', 'What is my place in the world?', 'What am I here for?') need to be *created*, just as *works of art* are created. For all practical intents and purposes, the question 'Can the life of every human individual become a work of art?' (or, more to the point, 'Can each and every individual be the artist of her or his life?') is purely rhetorical, the answer 'yes' being a foregone conclusion. Assuming that much, Foucault asks: if a lamp or a house can be a work of art, why not a human life?[3] I guess that both the 'new young' and the 'past generations' to whom Swida-Ziemba opposed them would have agreed wholeheartedly with Foucault's suggestions; but I also surmise that the people in each of the two cohorts compared by Swida-Ziemba would have had something different in their mind when thinking of 'works of art'.

Those of the past generations would probably have been thinking of something of lasting value, imperishable, resistant to the

flow of time and the caprices of fate. Following the habits of the
old masters, they would meticulously prime their canvases before
applying the first brushstroke, and equally carefully select the
solvents to make sure that the layers of paint wouldn't crumble
as they dried and would retain their freshness of colour over many
years to come, if not for eternity . . . The younger generation,
though, would seek the skills and patterns to imitate the practices
of currently celebrated artists – the 'happenings' and 'installations'. *Happenings*, of which one knows only that no one can be
sure what course they will eventually take (not even their designers, producers and prime actors), that their trajectory is a hostage
to ('blind', uncontrollable) fate, that as they develop anything may
happen but there is nothing that can be said to be certain to
happen. And *installations*, patched together from brittle and
perishable, preferably 'self-degradable' elements, since everyone
knows they won't survive the closure of the exhibition; in order
to make room for the next batch of exhibits, the gallery will need
to be cleared of the (now useless) bits and pieces – relics of the
old. The young may also associate works of art with the posters
and other prints they paste over the wallpaper in their room. They
know that the posters, just like the wallpaper, are not meant to
adorn their rooms forever. Sooner rather than later they will need
to be 'updated' – scraped off the wall to make room for the likeness of new idols.

Both generations ('past' and 'new') imagine works of art in the
likeness of the particular world whose true nature and meaning
the arts are presumed and hoped to lay bare and make available
to scrutiny. That world is expected to be made more intelligible,
perhaps even fully understood, thanks to the labours of artists;
but well before that happens, the generations who 'live through'
that world know or at least intuit its manners, so to speak, from
'autopsy' – from the personal experiences and the stories commonly told to report them and make them meaningful. No wonder,
then, that (in a stark opposition to previous generations) the young
believe that one can't really swear loyalty to the route designed
before the start of the life voyage, since random and unpredictable
fate and accidents my well redirect its itinerary. Of some of the
Polish young, Swida-Ziemba says that, for instance, 'they note
that a mate climbed high in the firm, was repeatedly promoted
and reached the top, until the company went bankrupt and he lost

everything he gained. It is for that reason that they may quit the studies which were going very well and go to England to work on a building site.' The others don't think of the future at all (it's a waste of time, isn't it?), don't expect life to reveal any logic except a stroke of luck (possibly) and banana skins on a sidewalk (equally probably) – and for that reason 'want every moment to be pleasurable'. Indeed: *every* moment. A non-pleasurable moment is a moment wasted. Since it is impossible to calculate what sort of future profits, if any, a present sacrifice may bring, why should one surrender the instant pleasures one can squeeze out from the 'here and now'?

The 'art of life' may mean different things to the members of older and younger generations, but they all practise it and can't possibly not. The course of life and the meaning of every successive life episode, as well as life's 'overall purpose' or 'ultimate destination', are nowadays presumed to be do-it-yourself jobs, even if they consist only in selecting and assembling the right type of flat-packed IKEA-style kit. Each and any practitioner of life is expected, just as artists are, to bear full responsibility for the outcome of the job and be praised or blamed for its results. Let me repeat: these days each man and each woman is an artist not so much by *choice* as, so to speak, *by the decree of universal fate*.

'Being artists by decree' means that non-action also counts as action; as much as swimming and navigating, allowing oneself to drift with the waves is a priori assumed to be an act of creative art and tends to be retrospectively recorded as such. Even those people who refuse to believe in the logical succession, continuity and consequentiality of their choices, decisions and undertakings, and in the feasibility and plausibility of their projects to tame fate, to overrule providence or destiny and to keep life on a steady, predesigned and preferred course – even they do not sit idly by; they still need to 'assist fate' by seeing to the endless little tasks which they are decreed by circumstances to perform as if following drawings attached to an assembly kit. Just as much as those who see no point in delaying satisfaction and decide to live 'for the moment', people who care for the future and are wary of undermining chances yet to come are convinced of the volatility of life's promises. They all seem to be reconciled to the impossibility of foolproof decisions, of predicting exactly which of innumer-

able successive steps will be (retrospectively!) shown to be the ones
rightly selected; or which of the haphazardly scattered seeds will
bring abundant and tasty fruit, and which buds will wilt and fade
before a sudden gust of wind or a wasp on a foraging escapade
has a chance to pollinate them. And so whatever else they believe,
they all agree that one needs to hurry; that doing nothing or doing
it slowly and lackadaisically is harmful.

Particularly the young, who, as Swida-Ziemba noted, collect
experiences and credentials 'just in case'. The young Poles say
'może'; the English of the same age would say 'perhaps', the French
'peut-être', the German 'vielleicht', the Italians 'forse', the Spanish
'tal vez' – but they would all mean much the same: who can know
whether one or the other ticket will win in the next life-lotto
draw? Only the unbought ticket has no chance of winning . . .

Excursus: Generations, then and now   It was not a mere contingency
that the category of 'generation' (in the sense of a totality with traits
that are common to all its units yet not to be found elsewhere) was born
and settled in social scientific as well as in public discourse in the after-
math of what was called the 'Great War' (and no wonder, as we will
see; only the first of the twentieth-century 'world wars' earned the name
of 'great', even if the Second World War left it far behind in territorial
reach, scale of devastation, goriness and the gravity of its consequences).
It was then that the seminal study of the intergenerational communication and conflicts was undertaken by Ortega y Gasset; and it was soon
afterwards that Karl Mannheim launched the newly discovered category, together with another conceptual newcomer, 'ideology', on their
amazing careers. One may say that the discovery of 'generation' in the
sense suggested by Ortega y Gasset and subsequently canonized by
Mannheim (that is, in the sense of a 'collective subject' marked by a
distinct worldview, as well as able to, and inclined to, act on its own
and in its own particular interests) was itself a generational achievement:
of the Great War generation.

Indeed, no wonder . . . Since the earthquake, fire and flood that
ravaged and destroyed Lisbon in 1755, the part of the planet that dubbed
itself 'civilization' had never experienced a mental and moral shock
comparable to that of the 'Great War'. The Lisbon catastrophe set the
budding 'modern civilization' at war with Nature, simultaneously
sapping and eventually supplanting the age-long trust invested in the
wisdom and intrinsic goodness and justice of Divine creation. It added
an overwhelmingly convincing, indeed clinching argument to the philosophers' insistence on the need to conquer Nature and subject it to

human management: to replace the blind randomness of Nature with a reason-guided, meticulously designed and monitored, accident-proof, predictable and above all manageable order, and so force it, under the new (human) administration, to serve properly human interests.

The 'Great War' catastrophe sapped that trust invested for almost two centuries in the wisdom and effectiveness of an order made by humans, based on science and technology, casting in doubt as well the conviction that such an order was bound to score higher in the goodness and justice it promoted than Nature was ever capable of doing. 'If', as Susan Neiman has suggested, 'Enlightenment [was] a courage to think for oneself, it [was] also the courage to assume responsibility for the world into which one is thrown' – but 'the more responsibility for evil was left to the humans, the less worthy the species seemed to take it on'.[4] What the 'Great War' had shown beyond reasonable doubt (and what was soon to be reconfirmed, if more confirmation was needed, by the wave of genocides that swept the planet) was that the results of human administration may be every bit as capricious, unpredictable, blind, thoughtless and indifferent to human virtues and vices as Nature stood accused of being two centuries earlier. And yet more atrocious and devastating.

The shock to the self-confidence, hubris and arrogance of the pioneers and spokesmen of 'civilization' must indeed have been overwhelming. Europe, after all, stepped into the twentieth century in a cloudlessly optimistic mood, the likes of which no one could remember. Everything or almost everything augured well, and better with each year. Vast expanses of lands and seas meekly surrendered to the will of Europe – and apparently dreamed of nothing other than to shake off the shackles of prejudice and embrace the triumphant creed of infinite progress preached by the gun-holding and bible-waving emissaries and missionaries of civilization. Scientists announced day in, day out the breaking of yet another alleged limit to human wisdom and potency. The life of many, if not as yet of all (only *as yet!*), became more comfortable and affluent with every passing year. Distances got shorter and less arduous, and time ran ever faster, so that ever more pleasurable gifts could be expected to be had and enjoyed in each of its units. The kingdom of Reason, the undivided rule of law and order – all that waited at the next corner. No one except a few evildoers or cranks aimed to resist the unstoppable march towards perfection, and anyone who harboured or nurtured such iniquitous intentions in secret was doomed to fail if they tried to follow odious thoughts with evil deeds. From the top to the bottom of society, people seemed to be getting more enlightened, even if not yet as willingly and expeditiously as could be wished and as surely would come about in the future. The evil passions of human beings

seemed to be ever more securely tamed, their mores getting gentler and
their cohabitation more peaceful; the will to resolve human disagreements by waging wars was gradually, yet visibly evaporating, replaced
by acceptance of the authority of reason and of the cause of the greater
happiness of ever greater numbers. History held firmly to the road it
had entered – or so it appeared. Changing direction was out of the
question, retreat was downright unthinkable.

To cut a long story short: the future of civilization was secure. Under
human management the world was safe and bound to get safer
still. Hans Habe, in his novel *Ilona,* vividly described the mood of
the time:

> People did not know what they were doing when, on New Year's
> Eve 1899, they celebrated the birth of the new century with jubila-
> tion. It was as though they were greeting the rain, not knowing
> that it was not going to cease until the rivers rose from their beds
> and turned the meadows into lakes and 'the waters rose fifteen
> cubits above the mountains'. They did not suspect that the waters
> would not fall upon a single day, but would rise gradually with
> the years. They did not suspect that the Lord God was tired of the
> twentieth century. They drank to the flood.

To the flood . . . Indeed, all of a sudden, taking everybody by surprise,
rivers rose from their beds and the flood started. The most massive
slaughter in human memory began. Deaths of millions in agonies
unheard of since the last heretic had been burned alive in the last dark
days of the Dark Ages. Cadavers riddled with bayonet wounds and
sliced by shrapnel splinters, crashed under the caterpillar tracks of tanks
and distended by gaseous poisons. Victims of hatred, prejudice and
superstition rotting alive for months on end in the swamps and quag-
mire of trenches, while envying the lucky ones whose deaths were merci-
fully instant. Together with its enlisted soldiers, civilization was dying
a slow, merciless, excruciatingly slow death in those trenches carved all
over Europe from the marshes of East Prussia to the waters of the
Somme; and dying together with civilization was the cosy homeliness
of the world for whose security it was believed to vouch. The safe world
sank and drowned, with no hope of resurrection, in the rivers of thought-
lessly and aimlessly spilt human blood.

All that horror was apparently born of a combination of a series of
accidents (for instance, the second bullet was released in Sarajevo by a
frustrated student because the driver of the royal coach mistook the road
to a hospital which the intended royal target of the first bullet wished
to visit in order to express his royal compassion to its accidental victim)

and a series of war plans, each worked out meticulously and with scientific precision by the top experts of the most advanced, most modern
and best-equipped armies of the most progressive corner of the planet
– all supremely rational and carefully calculated to make the hostilities
brief and nearly bloodless and to bring results as decisive as they would
be swift. What emerged, however, from that mixture of human planning
and man-made accidents did not appear in anybody's plans. *No one*
planned for this sort of an abattoir, for a mutual massacre four years
long – and this was perhaps the most shocking and horrifying of the
shocking and horrifying revelations of the Great War. That gruesome
event was *not* programmed, designed, anticipated, or even believed to
be conceivable. And the means selected to serve the *unplanned* tasks
proved wide of the mark and grossly ineffective; indeed, useless.

It was not that the calculations were revealed to be mistaken; erroneous calculations can be corrected, and correcting them may be a useful,
rationality-serving undertaking, since people tend to learn from their
mistakes, making their future less prone to accident and mischief. It was
rather the very idea that, given sufficient knowledge and technology, the
future can be calculated and goals secured by sharpening the means
that was consigned to the grave on the killing fields of the Somme,
Verdun and East Prussia – murdered and buried in the mass graves
alongside millions of soldiers, Europe's self-confidence, and the belief
of civilized people in the ultimate victory of reason over passions, their
trust in the wisdom and benevolence of history, and their comforting
feel-good conviction of a secure present and a guaranteed future.

It is not easy to reconstruct in full the trains of thought that led y
Gasset and Mannheim to focus their and their readers' attention on the
role played in history by generations. One can hypothesize nevertheless
that arriving at such a standpoint would have been much more difficult
for them if it had not been for the revelations of the Great War and the
'identity shock' they brought. If Paul Ricoeur split the phenomenon of
'identity' into two (*l'ipséité*, continuing distinctiveness from other
humans, and *la mêmeté*, continuing sameness with oneself), it was that
second part of identity that the Great War supplied with a huge question
mark. 'Myself' from before the Great War, 'myself' from after, and
'myself' spanning both the 'before' and the 'after' each spoke a different
language. All three could hardly find communication with the other two
easy. Could those who emerged alive from the slaughter fully understand, not to mention explain, the enthusiasm with which they had once
marched to the abattoir? And if they could, would they be able to convey
their new knowledge to ourselves of yore, cheering and dancing on
public squares on the day of mobilization? Could they comprehend how
it came about that what they knew now they could not imagine then,

and that in the unlikely event they had been offered it then they would have dismissed it outright as malicious whispers, and perhaps also lynched its messengers? And could they convey their comprehension, heavily paid for, to those born *after* Verdun and the Somme, apparently despairing at having missed 'the great test of manhood' and the 'most exciting' and 'character-forming' of adventures? And if they tried – would they be understood?

It seems probable that the blow delivered to *la mémété* of European identity was a decisive factor in promoting the notion of 'generation' to the rank of one of the main conceptual tools in the analysis of social and political divisions. The raw material for the *objective* analytical category was supplied by the *subjective* experience of a life cut into two strikingly dissimilar halves, mutually incommunicado. It seems probable as well that the laboratory in which the concept of generation was originally coined was the lived-through and lived-with opposition between 'us *now*' and 'us *then*'; distilled from the flasks of subjective experience and then reprocessed into a lens through which to scrutinize the world 'out there', that concept could be, and indeed was, deployed in drawing the lines separating 'us' from 'them'. The vision of intergenerational rupture and break in communication emerged in the effort to comprehend and 'make sense of' the experience of a personal fragmented life and to make intelligible the fracturing of time that disassembled the familiar *Lebenswelt* and made it vanish, replacing it with a world thus far unexplored and terrifying because of its unfamiliarity; a world all the more frightening for the absence of maps, and because of the prospect of preceding its mapping with a lengthy chain of random approaches, risky trials and potentially fatal errors.

Similar (though admittedly much more modest and less dramatic) subjective experiences of rupture were to recur, with rising frequency, as the flow of time accelerated and shortened the distance between successive avatars of the fast-changing human condition. No wonder that, once pinpointed and named, the issues of intergenerational divisions and the problems of intergenerational communication continue to arouse acute interest, losing nothing of their topicality. One may surmise that they have settled in scholarly and common vocabularies alike for a long time to come.

All the same, it is far from evident and remains by and large an open question whether in the current state of a genuinely permanent revolution, prompted by a compulsive and obsessive modernization of all aspects of human existence and a reversal of the ranks ascribed to transience and duration (or to immediacy and the long term) in the value hierarchy characteristic of the 'liquid' stage of the modern era, the notions under discussion have not forfeited some of their usefulness and ceased to serve properly the job of describing and comprehending the current human condition. One could argue that their continuing presence in our worldview may be a case similar to that of Ulrich Beck's 'zombie terms' (concepts alive in words but no longer in the flesh), or Jacques Derrida's terms allowed to be used solely *sous rature* (that is, inescapable for the communicative expediency of the narrative, but when used requiring a caveat/reminder that their worldly referents have already been deleted from the inventory of beings); I would say 'echo words', reverberating long after the crash that caused them has died down . . .

Indeed, the pace of change (at least inside our cultural area) is currently mind-boggling; changes are continuous and ubiquitous; and condensations of changes dense enough to justify drawing a new generational borderline seem either an almost daily, routine event, or on the contrary fewer and further between than ever (if we choose to compare their impact with that of the shock of the 'Great War'). Visible *changes* are numerous and crowded, increasingly seen and felt as permanent traits of the human condition, as ordinary rather than extraordinary events, the norm rather than an abnormality, a rule rather than an exception – whereas the *discontinuity of experience* is well-nigh universal and affects all age categories equally. Under such circumstances, drawing intergenerational borderlines can be only arbitrary, each attempt to do so must be controversial and contested, and their projection on to the map of society will not be particularly enlightening, if it is not misleading. Suggested divisions risk being the after-effects of the chosen method of processing statistical data, rather than reliable information about the morphology of the society described.

The pace of change perhaps tends to be too fast, and the speed with which new phenomena burst into public awareness and disappear from view too vertiginous. It bars the experience from crystallizing, settling and solidifying in attitudes and behavioural patterns, value syndromes and worldviews, fit to be recorded as durable traces of the 'spirit of the time' and recast as unique and lasting characteristics of a generation. In a crowd of scattered and apparently unconnected discontinuities, changes that can acquire the visibility and formative power of an 'upheaval' are few and far between. Few if any stand out enough to suggest a *generational* rupture and to provide the raw material for generational self-constitution and effective *self-assertion*.

To be recognized as an 'upheaval', a change needs to involve or provoke a wholesale and time-compressed 'revaluation of values' and a substantial rearrangement of the value hierarchy. Rules, norms and patterns until recently perceived as proper, effective and laudable must be recast as erroneous, useless and condemnable. As a result of such value reversal, the past as a whole, and particularly the part of the past still fresh in the public memory, will then be denigrated and subject to close (and hostile) interrogation. Each of its elements will come under suspicion and be considered guilty until proved innocent (though the innocence will almost never be proved beyond reasonable doubt, exoneration will never be complete – and suspicion will never be irrevocably put to rest). The sentence will be, at best, suspended – and that will apply as well to the verdicts pronounced in the past as not being subject to appeal. On the other hand, what used to be condemned or considered condemnable in the past will – in a similarly wholesale fashion and similarly a priori – be rehabilitated; the recognition denied in the past will be granted with few if any questions asked and no further proof of merit required.

All in all, in the event of a genuine 'upheaval' past evaluations are reversed only because they were voiced in the now disapproved of and deprecated 'past'. Virtues are rewritten as vices, achievements as misdeeds, loyalties as treachery – and vice versa. The devaluation of the valuations and practices of the past must be all the more decisive and uncompromising because the future, just taking off, is wrapped in mist. Nothing about its shape can be said with any confidence, except that it will be different from the past, and that few familiar landmarks will be on hand to mitigate the uncomfortable premonition of groping in the dark. In the absence of signposts showing the road ahead, perhaps reversing the signposts inherited from the past will do the trick – offering some, even if a purely negative, orientation, and some feeling, however flimsy and unreliable, of being in control of the eventual direction the course of forthcoming events will take. So it is no small an advantage that – although in the moment of upheaval any tested and trustworthy measures of future merits and accomplishments are unavailable (that is, measures which can be relied on to be still binding when the future turns into the present) – some substitute yet credible hierarchy of worthiness, and so also a form of meritocracy to fill the gap, can be composed right now by the simple expedient of renaming past demerits as merits, and vice versa.

'Upheavals' of such a sort are anomalies in our times. Or, rather, the other way round: turned into a daily diet, they are not exciting or frightening for more than a few days – until the advent of the next 'historic' or 'revolutionary' event is announced, with bated breath, by TV anchor-people and splashed all over the front pages of the tabloids, only to be wiped away shortly afterwards from the drifting attention of the public by another batch of 'sensational' and 'unprecedented' events. The idea of an 'upheaval' has become *trivialized* nowadays. In every copy of a glossy magazine there is something not about one, but about

quite a few things that were unheard of yesterday but which are bound
to be 'revolutionary' – to 'change the life' of some individuals in the
limelight, and so, by proxy, the life of everyone watching them.

On a slightly more serious note, the liquid modern world is in a state
of *permanent* revolution, a state that does not admit of the one-off,
'single event' revolutions remembered from the times of 'solid' modernity. If it is still permissible to speak of 'revolutions' today, then it is
only retrospectively – when, looking back, we realize that enough small
and apparently insignificant changes have accumulated to produce a
qualitative, not just an incremental transformation in the human condition. Deprived of its pristine referents, the idea of 'revolution' has been
trivialized: it is used and abused daily by writers of commercials,
introducing any 'new and improved' product as 'revolutionary' . . .

Amidst constant and ubiquitous changes, it is difficult, perhaps
impossible, to grasp correctly the 'upheavalist' nature of even the most
profound, but ongoing and incomplete transformations; it is even less
possible to design such transformations in advance and anticipate their
impact on the state of society. If a genuine upheaval does happen,
however, the life experiences that will sediment after the transformation
are certain to be sharply different from those remembered from before;
what for people on one side of the transformation was at best an exception, a breach in routine, will appear as a normal state of affairs for
those on the other side. The 'communicative turbulence' will then
become the first symptom of the emergent intergenerational divide. It is
not so much a 'conflict of interests' (an ideological gloss added at a later
stage to communicative trouble) as a disagreement concerning issues of
relevance and urgency, and problems arising from differently located,
non-overlapping areas of ignorance. The experiences essential for one
group have few or no referents in the experiences of another, whereas
issues of key importance to one group simply 'do not apply' to the other.

Mutual suspicion between generations, more often than not telescoped to form just two camps – 'the old' (or adults), and 'the young'
(not adults as yet, or reluctant to become adults) – has a long story. One
can easily trace its prodromal symptoms scattered over quite ancient
times; but it started in earnest in our modern era, once it had been
assumed that the world (or at least its human part) could be different
from what it was and that it was in the power of humans to make it
different; and once the world started changing quickly enough for 'it's
not what it used to be' to be noted in the course of a single human life
– and consequently for a gap to be visualized between 'what is' and
'what ought to be' and for concepts like 'the good old days' versus 'a
better future' to be coined and settled in philosophical meditations as
well as in the popular perceptions of life. It is then that people entering

the world at different stages of its continuous transformation might have started to *differ* sharply in the evaluation of the time they *shared*. What to some people might have seemed comfortable and cosy, since it allowed the deployment of skills and routines well learned and fully mastered, might have appeared odd and off-putting to others; whereas some people might have felt like fish in water in situations which made others feel ill at ease, baffled and at a loss. What by some might be seen as 'the way things are' or 'the way things are done' could be viewed by others as illegitimate, silly, unfair and altogether abominable.

As a result, the older and the younger age cohorts could eye each other with a mixture of miscomprehension and apprehension. The first would fear that the newcomers to the world were about to spoil and destroy what they, their elders, had preserved with loving care; the second would feel an acute urge to put right what the veterans had botched. Both would be unsatisfied with affairs as they stood and blame the others for their sorry state. In two consecutive issues of a highly respectable British weekly, two jarringly different charges were made public: a columnist accused 'the young people' of being 'bovine, lazy-arsed, chlamydia stuffed and good for nothing', to which a reader angrily responded that the allegedly slothful and uncaring youngsters are in fact 'academically high-achieving' and 'concerned about the mess that adults have created'.[5] Here, as in uncountable other similar disagreements, the difference is between evaluations suggested by experience-shaped viewpoints, and the resulting controversy can't be 'objectively' resolved.

Myself, I belong to one of those 'past generations'.

As a young man, together with most of my contemporaries, I read attentively the instructions of Jean-Paul Sartre concerning the choice of *le projet de la vie.* The choice of a 'life project' was meant to be the 'choice of choices', the meta-choice that would determine once and for all, from beginning to end, all the rest of the (subordinate, derivative, executory) choices. We learned from Sartre that to every project there would be attached a road map and a detailed description of the itinerary. Once the destination had been chosen, the rest would be just a matter of plotting the shortest and least hazardous road with the help of the map, a compass, and road signs . . .

We had no difficulty in understanding Sartre's message and found it chimed with what the world around appeared to announce or imply. In Sartre's world – the world shared by my generation –

maps aged slowly, if at all (some of them even boasted of being 'definitive'), roads once laid could be resurfaced from time to time to accommodate an increased number, weight and speed of vehicles, yet they would continue to lead to the same destination every time they were embarked on, and while the paint on the boards at junctions and on signposts might have been refreshed time and again, their messages never changed.

Again, in the company of other youngsters my age, I also listened patiently, with no murmur of protest let alone rebellion, to the lectures in social psychology founded on laboratory experiments with hungry rats in a maze as they sought the one and only 'right' succession of turns (that is, the one and only itinerary inside the labyrinth that led to a reward: an appetizing morsel of lard at its far end) in order to learn it and memorize it for the duration of their lives. We did not protest, because in the hubbub and tussle of laboratory rats, as much as in Sartre's advice, we heard our own life experiences echoing . . .

Most young people of today would certainly fail to recognize their own experience in the preoccupations of laboratory rats; they would also be likely to shrug their shoulders if they were advised to plot right away, at the start of the road, their whole life trajectory. Indeed, they would object: Do we know what the next month or year will bring? We can be certain of one thing only, they would rejoin: that the next month or year will be unlike the time we are living in now; that, being different, they will invalidate a lot of the knowledge we have now and much of the know-how we are currently using (though there is no guessing which part); that much of what we've learned we'll surely have to forget, while we'll have to get rid of many things of which we are proud and for which we are praised today (though again, there is no guessing which will have to go); and that the choices most recommended today may be decried tomorrow as shameful blunders. What follows (doesn't it, they would ask) is that the skill we really need to acquire first and foremost is *flexibility* (a neutered, and so currently politically correct, name for *spinelessness*) – the capacity to forget fast and promptly dispose of past assets that have turned into liabilities, as well as the ability to change tacks and tracks at short notice and without regret; and that what we really need to remember forever is the need to avoid swearing lifelong loyalty to anything and anybody. Good turns, after all, tend to appear suddenly and from nowhere, and vanish equally abruptly; woe to the suckers who, by design or default, behave as if they could hold on to them forever . . .

It seems these days that, although one can still dream of scripting a full-life scenario in advance, and even work hard to make the dream come true, to hold on to any scenario, even to the scenario of one's dream, is a risky matter and may yet prove suicidal. The scenarios of yore can date and fall out of use even before the play starts rehearsals, and if they manage to survive until the opening night the run of the play may still prove abominably brief. Having a whole stage of life (let alone the whole of life) committed to such a preconceived scenario will surely be equal to forfeiting the chance of many productions (there is no knowing how many . . .) which are more up to date, more in line with the current fashion, and for that reason more promising. New opportunities, after all, keep knocking – and there is no telling when and at which door they will knock.

Take, for instance, the case of Tom Anderson. Having studied art, he probably did not acquire much engineering know-how and had little notion of the workings of things technological. Like most of us, he was a user of modern electronics and, like most of us, must not have spent much time guessing and meditating on what was inside the computer box and how come that this rather than something else appeared on the screen when he pressed this rather than another key. And yet all of a sudden, probably to his own surprise, he was acclaimed in the computing world as the creator and pioneer of 'social networking' and the originator of what has been promptly dubbed 'the second internet revolution'. His blog, perhaps a mostly private pastime in its original intention, has evolved in less than a couple of years into the company MySpace, swarmed to by young and very young internauts (older web users, if they had heard of the new company and its fabulous popularity at all, perhaps played it down, or derided it as another passing fad or another silly idea with the life expectation of a butterfly). The 'company' was still bringing in no profit to speak of, and Anderson probably had no idea how to make it financially profitable (and probably no strong intention to do so either). Until July 2005, when Rupert Murdoch, unsolicited, offered 580 million dollars for the company that had survived until then on not much more than a shoestring . . . Murdoch's decision to buy MySpace

opened the sesames of this world much more aptly than the magic
of the most ingenious and sophisticated spells. Fortune scouts
promptly followed suit and invaded the web in search of uncut
diamonds. Yahoo bought another website in the 'social networking' category for a billion dollars, and in October 2006 Google
set aside 1.6 billion to obtain yet another, YouTube – begun just
a year and a half earlier, in a purely cottage industry fashion, by
another pair of amateur enthusiasts, Chad Hurley and Steve
Chene. On 8 February 2007 the *New York Times* informed us
that Hurley was paid Google shares worth 345 million dollars for
their felicitous idea, while Chene received shares with a market
value of 326 million.

'Being found' by Fate embodied in the person of a high and
mighty protector or a resourceful patron searching for as yet
unrecognized, or just not duly appreciated, talents has been a
popular motif in the biographical folklore of painters, sculptors
and musicians since the late Middle Ages and early Renaissance
(though not in the ancient world, where the arts were seen as ways
to depict, obediently and faithfully, the magic of Divine creation:
the Greeks 'could not reconcile the idea of creation under the
auspices of divine inspiration with monetary reward for the work
created'.[6] In antiquity, 'being an artist' was associated with renun-
ciation and poverty, with 'being dead to the world', rather than
with any kind of worldly, let alone pecuniary, success).

The etiological myth of 'being discovered' by a high and mighty
passer-by was only invented at the threshold of the modern era,
to account for the unprecedented cases (still few and far between)
of individual artists who suddenly rose to fame and riches in a
society which was known to regard birth as a life sentence with
no appeal allowed – and which had no room for the idea of a
self-made man (even less, of course, of a self-made woman); and
to account for these extraordinary cases in a way that would stubbornly reinforce and reaffirm, rather than undermine, the 'norm'
– the mundane order of power, might, authority, influence, and
the right to wealth and glory. Being of lowly origin, if not downright outcasts, future masters of the arts found as a rule (or so,
at least, the etiological myth insinuated) that even the divine gift
of the most sublime talents coupled with an uncommonly dogged
determination and a genuinely inexhaustible missionary zeal were
still not enough for them to fulfil their destiny, without a powerful

hand stretched out to lift them into the otherwise unreachable land of fame, riches and admiration.

Before the advent of modernity, the legend of 'meeting with Fate' was confined almost exclusively to artists; and no wonder, since the practitioners of what came later to be known as the 'fine arts', such as painters, sculptors, architects and composers, were almost the only people who managed to rise above their lowly station and end up supping with princes and cardinals, if not kings and popes. As modernity progressed, however, the ranks of the breakers of class barriers swelled.

As the numbers of 'parvenus' multiplied, so the stories inspired by 'meeting with Fate' were democratized. They now inform the life expectations of all and any of the *life* artists, mundane practitioners of the mundane arts of mundane life; and this means us all, or almost all. After all, nowadays we have all been decreed to stand a chance of 'meeting with Fate', of getting a stroke of luck or a run of luck which will lead to success and a life of happiness. If making our lives meaningful, successful and altogether happy depends on 'meeting with Fate', we are right to hope for, even to expect good fortune to come our way and ought to help it to do so – by stretching to the utmost our individual imagination and skilfully deploying all resources we manage to muster. By, in other words, leaving no *chance* unturned . . .

True, it is mostly the practitioners of the fine arts (or, more precisely, those not too numerous, lucky people whose practices, courtesy of a sudden award of celebrity status, have been classified as 'fine arts' with no further argument) whose fables of a miraculous rise from rags to riches are bathed in limelight and publicly applauded and admired. For instance, the story of a girl who used to sell for 2 pounds apiece glass ashtrays worth 50 pence, adorned with photographs of pop idols cut out pell-mell from newspapers and glued to the bottom in a slapdash manner . . . a girl biding her time in a drab little shop on a drab little street in East London – until one day a limousine stopped in front of that shop carrying a great art patron destined to transform her unmade bed into a priceless work of high art in the manner of the fairy godmother of Cinderella-story fame, fabled to conjure up a carriage dripping with gold out of a pumpkin . . .

Stories of the masters of fine art (or, more precisely, of boys and girls magically transformed into such) have the advantage of falling on a ground well prepared by the centuries-old tradition of story-telling. They fit particularly well in the mood of our *liquid modern* times because, unlike the *early modern* stories (for instance, the notorious legend of a shoeshine boy turned million-aire), they keep silent about the awkward, thorny and rather off-putting issues of patience, hard work and self-sacrifice that success in life was previously thought to require. The presently popular stories of celebrated visual or performing artists play down the issue of the *kind* of activity to which one applies oneself and the *way* in which one does so; in a liquid modern world, after all, no worthy activities retain their worthiness for long. It is, rather, the general principle on which the typically liquid modern stories focus: that in a compound with benevolent fate any haphazardly added ingredient, however common it might be, plain and unim-pressive, can cause the glittering crystals of success to sediment from the murky solution called 'life'. *Any* ingredient: not neces-sarily the drudgery, self-denial, asceticism or self-sacrifice sug-gested by the classic-modern stories.

Under such conditions, the invention of computerized networks came in eminently handy. One of the many virtues of the internet (and one of the principal causes of the mind-boggling pace of its growth: the number of internet users, still negligible in 1997, is projected to pass the 2.5 billion mark in 2010, while e-mail traffic alone produced in one year (2006) 20 per cent – one exabyte – more information than 'all human language since the dawn of time would carry'[7]) is that it puts paid to the awkward necessity of taking sides in the ancient, now resented and out-of-fashion oppositions between work and leisure, exertion and rest, purpose-ful action and idleness, or indeed application and sloth. The hours spent in front of your computer as you zap your way through the thicket of websites – what are those hours spent on? Work or entertainment? Labour or pleasure? You won't tell, you don't know, and frankly you don't care – and you have to be absolved from the sins of your ignorance and indifference, since the reliable answer to those dilemmas will not come and cannot come until fate shows its hand.

It is little wonder therefore that, by 31 July 2006, 50 million blogs had been counted on the world wide web, and that accord-ing to later calculations their numbers have grown since then by an average of 175 thousand a day. About what do those blogs inform the 'internet public'? About everything that occurs to their owners/authors/operators (there is no knowing what, if anything, may suddenly attract the attention of the Rupert Murdochs or Charles Saatchis of this world . . .). Creating a 'personal site', a blog, is just another variety of a lotto: you go on buying tickets 'just in case', with or without the illusion that there are rules that enable you (or anyone else for that matter) to predict the winning ones; at least the kind of rules you could learn and remember in order to faithfully, and to good effect, observe them in your practice. Jon Lanchester, who examined a large number of blogs, found one blogger reporting in great detail what he had consumed for breakfast, another describing the joys of the previous evening's game, a female blogger complaining of the intimate and secret shortcomings of her partner, another blogger displaying an ugly photograph of the author's pet dog, yet another meditating on the discomforts of a policeman's life and another still collating the tastier bits of the sexual exploits of an American in China.[8] And yet one trait could be found that was shared by all or almost all the blogs, however their contents might have varied: an unashamed sincerity and straightforwardness in displaying in public the most private experiences and most intimate adventures. Brutally speaking, an evident lack of inhibition in putting oneself (or at least some parts or aspects of one's self) on the market. Perhaps one item or another might make an important surfer-by pause and look closer; perhaps it might inflame the imagination of a prospective buyer, even of some rich and powerful buyer – or perhaps just of ordinary surfing folk, but enough of them to attract the attention of the powerful few and inspire them to make the bloggers an offer they couldn't refuse, pushing their market price sky high? Public confessions (the juicer the better) of the most personal and supposedly secret affairs are a sort of 'substitute currency' which can be resorted to by those who can't afford the currencies routinely used by more 'serious' (read: more resourceful) investors. There is little point in the art of life unless there is some hope, if only a hazy one, that the *objets d'art* it produces will be admired – on the streets and public squares, or in the intimacy of someone's boudoir or computer room . . .

Many learned art critics suggest that the arts have nowadays conquered the whole world of the living. The allegedly idle dreams of the last century's avant-garde have been fulfilled – though not necessarily in the form they wished and hoped their victory to take. It seems that once they are victorious, the arts may no longer need the art-works to manifest their existence.

Not so long ago, and most certainly in the halcyon days of the avant-garde, the arts strove to prove their right to survive by trying to document their usefulness to the world and its inhabitants. They needed to leave behind solid and durable traces of their accomplishments, hard proof of the valuable services they render – tangible and possibly irremovable traces and indestructible proof, promising to last forever; now, however, they not only manage well without solid traces of their presence, but all too often seem to be careful not to threaten to outstay their welcome and so avoid any traces that are too deep for a speedy and expedient effacement. The arts of the present day appear to specialize mostly in a quick assembly and prompt dismantling of their creations; at least, they treat the assembly and disassembly as equally valid, worthy and indispensable forms of artistic creativity. One acclaimed American artist, Rauschenberg, put on sale sheets of paper on which drawings had once been made by another famous American artist, de Kooning, but from which he had laboriously, though not completely, effaced almost all pencil traces; his own, Rauschenberg's, creative contribution, for which collectors were expected to pay, was traces of rubbing out. By the same token, Rauschenberg promoted *destruction* to the rank of artistic *creation*; it was the act of *annihilating* the traces left on the world, not *imprinting* them, that his gesture was aimed at representing as the valuable service the arts offer their contemporaries. In sending such a message, he was by no means alone among the most prominent and influential contemporary artists: recall, for instance, Gustav Metzger, the pioneer of 'self-destructive art' and convenor of the 1966 symposium on destruction as art. The obliteration of traces, or covering up tracks, was and continues to be placed at the level hitherto occupied solely by the embossing and engraving of those marks, or otherwise making them salient – preferably permanently. This happens, too, at that other level – of the life arts – where the most urgently needed tools of life are experimented with and the gravest challenges of the human existential condition are located, confronted and dealt with.

Indeed, everything said above about the recent transformation of the fine arts applies in full to the arts' most common, univer-

sally practised genre: the art(s) of *life*. In fact, the fateful depar-
tures that have occurred and continue to occur in the fine arts
seem to have resulted from the efforts of the artists to catch up
with the changes in the art of life, or at least in its most ostenta-
tiously displayed varieties. As in so many other respects, so in this
case, the fine arts *replicate* life; in most cases, new currents in the
fine arts follow, with some delay, changes in the mode of life –
even if their creators do their best to anticipate these changes
and sometimes succeed in inspiring or facilitating a change and
smoothing its entry into the practices of daily life. Before the
artists discovered it, 'creative destruction' was already widely
practised and entrenched in mundane life as one of its most
common, indeed routinely applied expedients. Rauschenberg's
gesture could be interpreted as an attempt to update the meaning
of 'representative painting' . . . Any professional and aspiring
artist who wishes to lay bare, put on display and render intelligible
human experiences (in both their *Erfahrungen* and *Erlebnisse*
forms), anyone who wants their oeuvres to faithfully represent
those experiences, needs to follow Metzger's manifesto and
Rauschenberg's example of unmasking, making salient and available to scrutiny the intimate connections between creation and
destruction . . .

To practise the art of life, to make one's life a 'work of art',
amounts in our liquid modern world to being in a state of permanent transformation, to perpetually self-redefine through becoming (or at least trying to become) *someone other* than one has
been thus far. 'Becoming someone else' amounts, however, to
ceasing to be who one has been thus far; to breaking and shaking
off one's old form as a snake shakes off its skin or a shellfish its
carapace; to rejecting, one by one, the used-up personae – shown
by the steady flow of 'new and improved' opportunities on offer
to be worn out, too tight or just not as fully gratifying as they
have been in the past. To put a new self on public display and
admire it in a mirror and in the eyes of others, one needs to
remove the old self from one's own and other people's sight, and
possibly also from one's own and their memory. When engaged
in 'self-defining' and 'self-asserting', we practise *creative destruction*. Daily.

To many people, particularly to young ones who have left
behind only a few traces, mostly shallow and easy to obliterate,

this new edition of the art of life may well appear attractive and likeable. Admittedly, not without good reason. This new kind of art promises a long, seemingly infinite string of future joys. It promises in addition that the seeker of a joyful, satisfying life will never suffer an ultimate, definitive, irrevocable defeat, that after every setback there will be a second chance and a possibility to recover, with permission to cut their losses and 'start again', 'begin from the (new) beginning' – or even win back or fully compensate for what was lost in the act of 'being born again' (read: through joining another, and hopefully more user-friendly and lucky, 'only game in town'), so that the destructive bits in the successive acts of creative destruction can be easily forgotten and the bitter aftertaste of loss can be quashed by the sweetness of new vistas and their yet untested promises.

In the times already recalled when Jean-Paul Sartre proposed that the consistent fulfilment of the 'life project' was the essence of the art of life, successive life situations and their challenges did not appear to people as self-sustaining and self-contained episodes. Rightly or wrongly, they were perceived as *stages* of a pre-designed itinerary, arranged one after another in a strict, 'natural', perhaps even preordained order; something akin to rosary beads, strung in a predetermined, non-negotiable and unalterable succession which anyone telling their beads must obligingly follow.

From the first moment and until the end of life, according to the way suggested by Sartre, the trajectory of life would proceed through an itinerary designed well before the first step was taken. Sartre's *projet de la vie* was a secular equivalent of the road to salvation, of life as a pilgrimage to the crossroads between eternal grace and eternal damnation – except that in their secular version, grace, redemption and salvation had no use for an other-worldly life; in the secular version, the pilgrimage together with its final destination were wholly inserted and contained in the bodily life of this world. But both versions, the secular equivalent as much as its religious original, presented life as a *pilgrimage* to a destination designated *once and for all*; and both versions assumed that once the destination was chosen, exact instructions on how to reach it could be obtained and learned. What was left to the pilgrim and remained his responsibility was only the duty to follow the route faithfully, resisting the temptation of putative short cuts, of the roads that were more scenic or paths that were easier to walk.

Persistent, determined and tough people may still set their hearts and minds on following Sartre's suggestion; but knowing that they've chosen a daunting task with no guarantee, or even a reasonably realistic hope, of it being seen through, they must be aware that the task is indeed daunting. They must weigh the strength of their dedication against the severity of the tests they are likely to face and against the extent of sacrifices which the passing of the tests is likely to require. Such people (just like the rest of us) must be aware that for the duration of the pilgrimage the travelling conditions are bound to remain much as they appear to be today: marked by an incurable fragility of social positions and sources of living, a brittleness of interhuman bonds, a chameleon-like mutability of coveted values and of those matters recommended by public opinion as worthy of attention and effort; as if everything around colludes to make the life of devoted pilgrims difficult and off-putting, and to punish them for their obstinacy and loyalty to the decision once taken.

Let me recall as well that the men and women whose life experience Sartre fathomed and to whom he addressed his message were taught psychology based on the exploits of laboratory rats forced to find, learn, memorize and follow 'from now to eternity' the one and only way through a maze that similarly promised 'from now to eternity' the coveted reward. In other words, the life task of the rats was assumed to consist in learning in order to *adjust*, and in adjusting in order to *survive* – by adapting their conduct to the non-negotiable shape of an orderly, solid and imperturbable world. If, however, psychology were still to be taught today deriving its wisdom from experiments with rats in a maze, and were its teachers to hope that their students might accept it as a fair reflection of their world and a model relevant to their own life experience, the partitions inside the maze would need to be put on castors and moved around from one trial to another, whereas the prizes for reaching the goal would need to be placed in a new and always unexpected place in every round. But then the very idea of life as a lasting, once-and-for-all adaptation to the lasting, once-and-for-all demands of the world that underpinned the deployment of rats' experience to instruct future practitioners of human lives would appear to them as much as to their students nebulous, if not altogether absurd and ludicrous.

In a world like ours, a world in which any target believed to
be worth pursuing appears in sight for only a brief moment, often
in places not hitherto known to be promising and worthy of visiting, or (worse still) in places in which roads successfully walked
in the past and so deemed to be well tested may now lead one
astray, the planning of long-term escapades is bound to be a risky
affair. Not many people, and only people endowed with rather
uncommon qualities, will be likely to undertake the risk willingly
and accept the high probability of defeat. A world bristling with
traps and ambushes favours and rewards short cuts, projects that
can be completed in a short time, targets that can be hit immediately. It also encourages an 'enjoy now and pay later' attitude,
while discouraging reflections and worries of the 'what does it all
amount to' kind. It is as if the thread holding the rosary beads
together has been cut, and the beads have scattered all over the
place, so that it does not matter any longer which one is fingered
first; the 'rational' way to proceed is to catch the one which
happens to be the nearest at the moment and can be caught with
the least effort and delay.

As in the case of 'smart' missiles (as opposed to their ballistic
predecessors), the targets to be given priority for action according
to the strategy of instrumental rationality are seldom chosen
before launch; they tend to emerge (if at all) as afterthoughts, at
the other end of the action, as their unanticipated consequences.
Rather than informing and determining the action as its motive,
the 'objective' of action tends to be searched for, found or con-
strued retrospectively, at the far end of the string of events.

Paradoxically, pressure is most difficult to resist, fight back against
and repel when it does not resort to blatant coercion and does not
threaten violence. The command 'you must do it (or you mustn't
do it), or else' prompts resentment and breeds rebellion. On the
other hand, a suggestion that 'you want it, you deserve it, you
owe it to yourself, you can get it, so go for it' panders to an *amour
de soi* constantly hungry for compliments. It nourishes a perpetually unsatiated self-esteem and encourages the exploration of the
unexplored . . .

In our society of consumers, the urge to replicate the style of
life currently recommended by the latest market offers and praised
by paid or voluntary market spokespeople – and so also, by impli-

cation, the compulsion to perpetually overhaul one's identity and public persona – have ceased to be associated with *coercion* (an *external* coercion, and for that reason particularly offensive and annoying). They tend to be perceived, on the contrary, as manifestations of (flattering and gratifying) *personal freedom*. Only if a person tries to opt out and retreat from chasing after an elusive, forever unfinished identity, or if they are blackballed and driven away from the chase or refused admission a priori, will they learn how limited that freedom is – how powerful are the forces which own and/or manage the racetrack, guard the entrances and prod the runners into running; and only then will that person find out how severe is the punishment meted out to the hapless and/or insubordinate. That this is the case is known only too well by people who lack a bank account and credit cards and can't afford the price of entry. Many others still can sense the spectre of all such horrors from the dark premonitions that haunt them in the nights following the busy selling and buying days – or, yet more tangibly, from the red alerts that follow when the bank account falls into the red or the credit available falls to zero.

The road signs marking the trajectories of life appear and vanish with little warning. Maps of territory likely to be crossed at some point in the future need to be updated almost daily – and are, albeit irregularly and without notice. Maps are printed and put on sale by many publishers and available in profusion in any newsagent, but none of them is 'authorized' by an office credibly claiming control over the future; by whatever map you decide to orient your movements, you do it at your own risk and responsibility. In short, the life of the seekers/constructors/reformers of identity is anything but short of trouble; their particular art of life demands a great deal of money, unremitting effort and, on many an occasion, nerves of steel. No wonder that despite all the joys and blissful moments it promises and at one time or another delivers, quite a few people hesitate to view such a life as the kind of life they would continue to practise given genuine liberty of choice.

It is often said of such hesitant people that they are indifferent, if not downright hostile, to freedom, or that they have not grown up and matured enough to enjoy it . . . Which implies that non-participation in the style of life dominant in the liquid modern society of consumers tends as a rule to be explained either by an

ideologically inspired resentment of freedom, or by ineptitude in
using its gifts and blessings. Such an explanation, however, is at
best only partially true.

The volatility, vulnerability and frailty of every and any identity
burdens the identity-seeker with the duty of attending daily to the
chores of *identification*. What might have started as a conscious
undertaking can turn, in the course of time, into a routine no
longer reflected upon, whereby the endlessly and ubiquitously
repeated assertion that 'you *can* make yourself into someone other
than you are' is rephrased as 'you *must* make yourself into someone
other than you are'. 'You must' does not resonate with the promised and expected freedom, and it is out of their sincere desire for
freedom that many people might rebel against it. Whether or not
you possess the substantive resources demanded by 'doing what
you must', this 'must' sounds more like slavery and oppression
than any imaginable avatar of liberty. Meat for some, poison for
(many? most?) others, but a mixture of nourishment and poison
for all. If 'to be free' means to be able to act on one's wishes and
pursue one's chosen objectives, the liquid modern, consumerist
version of the art of life may *promise* freedom to all, but it *delivers* it sparingly and selectively. Just to make a life of perpetual
precariousness liveable, a considerable margin of the 'precariat',
as Loïc Wacquant calls them, are compelled to form their 'subjectivity' out of (hostile) objectifications (stereotyping) by others.
Their 'advanced marginality'

> tends to concentrate in isolated and bounded territories increas-
> ingly perceived by both outsiders and insiders as social purgator-
> ies, leprous badlands at the heart of the postindustrial metropolis
> where only the refuse of society would accept to dwell.[9]

In an insightful study of philosophical reflections on the art of
life, Alexander Nehamas reveals and tries to explain the mysteri-
ous fascination of European philosophers with the person of
Socrates;[10] or rather with the colourful portrayal of his uncommon style of life left by Xenophon and Plato; Socrates himself did
not record any of the thoughts immortalized by those two authors.
Socrates refrained from confessing the reasons why he became
what he was. As Nehamas puts it, Socrates was 'stubbornly silent
about himself'.

Notwithstanding numerous sharp and profound differences in their perceptions of the world and the task of philosophy, as well as in their political sympathies and values, the most powerful minds of the modern era and legions of their followers were in agreement in selecting Plato's Socrates as a model of the meaningful and dignified life. Moreover, they all singled him out for much the same reason: they chose Socrates (and particularly the Socrates of the *early* dialogues of Plato) because this ancient sage and forefather of modern thought was fully and truly a 'self-made man', a pastmaster of self-creation and self-assertion, and yet he never presented his own chosen way of being as the sole model of the worthy way of life which all other humans ought to emulate (it was only in his late dialogues, starting from the *Apology*, that in a sudden about-face Plato moved to recommend for universal imitation not just the *consistency* with which Socrates held to the path he chose, but also *the choice* itself; but as Nehamas points out, siding with widespread opinion among Plato scholars, the arguments summoned by Plato to convince his readers that a Socrates-like dedication to philosophy was the only recipe for a decent life were as unconvincing as they were weak or flawed, and relatively easy to counter). For the great modern philosophers who recommended Socrates as a model to follow, to 'imitate Socrates' meant to compose *one's own* self, personality and/or identity, freely and *autonomously*; not to copy the personality Socrates created for himself, or any other personality, whoever might have composed and practised it. The meaning of living one's life 'the Socratic way' was *self*-definition and *self*-assertion and a readiness to accept that life cannot be other than a work of art for whose merits and shortcomings the 'auctor' (actor and author rolled into one; the designer and simultaneously the executor of the design) bears full and sole responsibility.

'To imitate Socrates' meant, in other words, to staunchly *refuse* imitation; refuse imitation of the person 'Socrates' – or any other person, however worthy. The model of life Socrates selected, painstakingly composed and laboriously cultivated for himself might have perfectly suited his kind of person, but it would not necessarily suit all those who made a point of living as Socrates did. A slavish imitation of the specific mode of life that Socrates constructed on his own, and to which he remained unhesitatingly, steadfastly loyal throughout, would amount to a *betrayal* of his legacy, to the *rejection* of his message – a message calling people first and foremost to listen to their own reason, and calling thereby for individual autonomy and *responsibility*. Such an imitation could suit a copier or a scanner, but it will never result in an original artistic creation, which (as Socrates suggested) human life should strive to become . . .

Just like painters or sculptors, we – practitioners, by default if not by design, of the art of life – will not settle for just any artistic creation (just any model of life). We all, or at least most of us, tend to seek something special – unique and superb, indeed an 'absolute': an 'ultimate' model, a model better than all other models, a *perfect* model, a model so good that it can't be improved further since nothing 'better' can exist or be imagined. We tend to strive after a model that will entail all the good things the good life needs and can entail – a model which, for those reasons, will surpass, dwarf and devalue all alternatives. The model we are after would probably not pass the philosophical test of universal validity – but for us, its seekers, it does not stop short of the *absolute*.

Tzvetan Todorov warns that the all too common pitfalls which the seekers of the 'Absolute' are likely to encounter are strikingly similar to the devious paths on to which the seekers of love are all too often diverted.[11] In stark opposition to widespread yet misguided beliefs and expectations, the 'Absolute', just like love, does not wait for its discoverer ready-made and ready for use. The 'Absolute' needs to be *created* and have life breathed into it – and not just in a *one-off* act of creation; it can exist only in a state of *permanent* creation, it needs to be constantly *re*created, day by day and hour after hour. Absolutes are not *found*; they are *made*. They exist solely in the modality of *being made*. The value and attractiveness of the Absolute dreamed of by identity-seekers lies, whether they know it or not, in the labour of self-creation.

True, it may happen that one comes across a near-absolute perfection (as with a near-perfect love) by accident. It may happen, though not too often, that like other works of art striving for perfection, the dreamed-of Absolute can start its life as a sort of 'found object'. Any weakening of dedication and vigilance and any slackening of attention and care, however, could cause its (similarly 'accidental') loss. There is as much (and no more) holding power in an 'absolute value' chosen to serve as our life guide and the supreme judge of what our life has produced, as there is obstinacy in our dedication, lasting determination in our choice, and persistence in our effort.

Todorov made his choice, and with enough confidence to recommend it to his (unknown) readers. In his view, the most satisfaction of the type that a successful work of art is able, and expected, to offer can be derived from a life attaining, or at least steering nearer to, Truth, Beauty, Goodness, Love; in other words, a life approaching the universal categories deemed to be worthy of desire and diligent effort thanks not to their instrumental uses, but to their very nature. Paradoxically however, and despite our assumptions and verbal declarations (assumptions we can't do without lest the categories at issue forfeit their magnetic power; and declarations we are obliged to make if we wish our choices to gain social approval), what we are after in this case is an '*individual* Absolute'. This is an oxymoron to be sure, a logical impossibility, in as far as the 'Absolute' is by definition *universal*, and so *supra*-individual and in this sense *im*personal; an 'individual absolute' is therefore contrary to logic . . . Whether or not they are burdened with an inner contradiction that should, according to the principles of logic, disqualify them, it is precisely 'individual absolutes' (*individually* chosen and *individually* lifted to the rank of supreme value on the *individual* responsibility of the chooser) that allow us, as Todorov intimates, to set apart a captivating, endearing, joyful, truly sense-filled and sense-filling life from a life which is a collection of trashy trinkets and fleeting amusements.

Whichever way you look, reflection on the art of life leads in the last resort to the idea of *self*-determination and *self*-assertion, and to the strong will that facing up to such a daunting task necessarily requires.

As Max Frisch, the great novelist and no lesser philosopher of life, noted in his diary, the art of 'being yourself', arguably the most demanding of all the arts, consists in resolutely rejecting and repelling definitions and 'identities' imposed or insinuated by others; in resisting the current, escaping the incapacitating grip of Heidegger's impersonal *das Man*, born of the crowd and powerful through the crowd, or Sartre's *l'on*; in short – in 'being someone else' and not what external pressures coerce everyone to be. Frisch's rich literary oeuvre (see particularly his novels *Homo*

Faber, Stiller, or *For Instance, Gantenbein)* can be read as exten-
sive, fictionalized commentaries on that assertion.

In a remarkable synthesis of the life experiences most common in
our individualized society, François de Singly lists the dilemmas
that tend to cast each of the individual practitioners of the art of
life into a state of acute and incurable uncertainty and perpetual
hesitation.[12] Life pursuits cannot but oscillate between mutually
incompatible, even starkly opposite targets, like, for instance,
joining and opting out, imitation and invention, routine and spontaneity – all these oppositions being only exemplifications of the
meta-opposition, the supreme opposition in which individual life
is inscribed and from which it is unable to cut itself free: the
opposition between *security* and *freedom*, both ardently coveted
but excruciatingly difficult to reconcile, and virtually impossible
to be fully satisfied at the same time.

The product of the art of life is supposed to be the 'identity' of
the artist. But given the oppositions which self-creation struggles
in vain to reconcile, and the interplay between the constantly
changing world and the similarly unstable self-definitions of individuals trying hard to catch up with changing life conditions,
identity can't be internally consistent; nor can it at any point
exude an air of finality which implies there is no room (and
prompts no urge) for further improvement. Identity is perpetually
in statu nascendi; each of the forms it successively assumes tends
to be afflicted by a more or less acute inner contradiction. Each
form fails to a greater or lesser extent to satisfy, each yearns for
reform, and each lacks the trustworthiness that could only be
achieved by a comfortingly long life expectation.

As Claude Dubar suggests, 'identity is nothing other than the
result – simultaneously stable and provisional, individual and
collective, subjective and objective, biographical and structured
– of diverse processes of socialization which at the same time
construct the individuals and define the institutions.'[13] We may
observe, however, that the 'socialization' itself, contrary to opinions universally held not so long ago and still frequently expressed,
is *not* a one-directional process, but a complex and unstable
product of an ongoing interplay between the yearning for individual freedom of self-creation and an equally strong desire for
security which only the stamp of social approval, countersigned

by a community (or communities) of reference, can offer. The tension between the two is seldom placated for long, and hardly ever vanishes altogether.

De Singly rightly suggests that in theorizing about present-day identities, it would be better if the metaphors of 'roots' and 'uprooting' (or, let me add, the related tropes of 'embedment' and 'disembedment') – implying a one-off act of individual emancipation from the tutelage of the community of birth and the finality, irreversibility of that act – were abandoned and replaced by the tropes of the casting out and drawing up of *anchors*.[14]

Indeed, unlike in the case of 'uprooting' and 'disembedding', there is nothing irrevocable, let alone ultimate, in drawing up an anchor. When they are torn out of the soil in which they grew, roots are likely to desiccate, killing the plant they nourished and making its revival border on the miraculous – anchors are drawn up only to be cast out again, and they can be cast out with similar ease at many different, near or distant ports of call. Besides, roots design and determine in advance the shape to be assumed by the plants growing out of them; roots exclude the possibility of any other shape. But anchors are only facilities serving an explicitly temporary attachment to or detachment from the place, and in no way do they define the ship's features and qualities. The stretches of time separating the casting out of an anchor from drawing it up again are just phases in the ship's trajectory. The choice of haven where the anchor is to be cast next is most probably determined by the kind of load the ship is currently carrying; a haven good for one kind of load may be entirely inappropriate for another.

All in all, the metaphor of anchors captures what the metaphor of 'uprooting' misses: the intertwining of continuity and discontinuity in the history of all or at least of a growing number of contemporary identities. Just like ships mooring successively or intermittently at various ports of call, so the selves in the 'communities of reference' (to which they seek admission during their lifelong journey in search of recognition and confirmation of their identity) have their credentials checked and approved at every successive stop; each 'community of reference' sets its own requirements for the kind of evidence to be submitted. The ship's record and/or the captain's log are more often than not among the documents on which the approval depends, and with every next stop, the past (constantly swelled by the records of preceding stops) is re-examined and revalued.

There are of course ports, as there are communities, which are not too pedantic in checking credentials and care little about the past, present or future destinations of their visitors; they will admit virtually any ship (or any 'identity'), including ships which would probably be turned away at the entrance to most other ports (or at the checkpoints of any other community). But then visiting such ports (and such 'communities') carries little 'identifying' value and is better avoided, since depositing precious loads there might prove to be a liability some time in the future rather than an asset. Paradoxically, the emancipation of the self needs strong, choosy and demanding communities as its tools.

Self-*creation* is a must, and indeed an unavoidable accomplishment, but the idea of self-*affirmation* feels more like a sheer figment of the imagination (and is widely decried as a case of autism or self-delusion). And what difference would all that effort invested in self-creation make to the individual's standing, confidence and capacity to act were affirmation, its finishing act and purpose, not to follow? But affirmation capable of completing the labour of self-creation can be offered only by an *authority*: a community whose *admission counts* because *it has the power to refuse admission* . . . Even the most original itineraries cannot but be lists of successive ports of call.

'Belonging', as Jean-Claude Kaufmann suggests, is today 'used primarily as a resource of the ego'.[15] He warns against thinking of 'collectivities of belonging' as necessarily 'integrating communities'. They are better conceived of as necessary accompaniments to the process of individualization; as a series of stations, we may say, or inns on the road, marking the trajectory of the self-forming and self-reforming ego.

'Integrating community' is a notion inherited from the now bygone 'panoptical' era: it refers to organized efforts to neatly draw and fortify the borderline separating 'us' from 'them', the 'inside' from the 'outside'; efforts to keep the inmates inside while barring outsiders from entry and the *insiders* from breaching norms and loosening the grip of routine. All in all, it refers to promoting uniformity and the enforcement of a straitjacket on conduct. The notion suggests restrictions imposed on movement and change: 'integrating community' is essentially a conservative (conserving, stabilizing, routine-imposing and preserving) force. It is at home in a strictly administered, tightly supervised and policed setting – hardly in the liquid modern world with its cult of speed and acceleration, novelty and change just (or mostly) for the sake of changing.

Today, panoptical instruments in their traditional form inherited from the 'solid modern' past are deployed mostly at the social periphery – to bar the re-entry of the excluded to the company of bona fide members of the society of consumers, and to keep the *outcasts* out of mischief. What is currently mistaken for an updated version of Orwell's 'Big Brother' or Jeremy Bentham's 'Panopticon' is in fact the very opposite of the alleged originals: a contraption deployed in the service of *exclusion* and 'keeping out', not of 'integration', 'keeping in' and 'keeping in line'. It monitors the movement of *outsiders* to prevent them from turning into or pretending to be insiders – so that the insiders can feel comfortable inside, and feeling comfortable can be relied on to follow internal rules with less surveillance and no enforcement.

The supra-individual entities to which 'mainstream' individuals offer their allegiance at some stage of their life itinerary, only to withdraw it at the next stop or the stop after next, are anything but the *integrating* communities of the past: they do not monitor the human traffic at their fringes, do not register those crossing borders in either direction, and are hardly aware of individual decisions to 'join' or 'leave' – and they do not run offices that could engage in all that monitoring, registration and recording. Rather than integrating those currently 'belonging', these entities are brought into being and 'kept whole' (though in an admittedly loose and easily arrested and reversible manner) by the decisions of individuals to 'join' and 'follow the pattern'; from the moment such decisions begin to be taken until massive desertion begins.

There is another seminal difference between the forms and tokens of contemporary 'belonging' and the orthodox 'integrating communities'. To quote Kaufmann once more, 'a large part of the identification process feeds on rejection of the Other'.[16] Access to one group is simultaneously an act of resignation or retirement from another: selecting a group as a site of belonging constitutes some other groups as foreign and potentially hostile territory : 'I am P' means (at least implicitly, but often explicitly) that 'I am *not* Q, R, S, etc.'. 'Belonging' is one side of the coin of which the other side is separation and/or opposition – all too often breeding intergroup resentment, antagonism and open conflict. The above applies to all instances of 'belonging', of access and offers of allegiance. But in the course of the modern era this universal feature has undergone significant modifications with the passage from *identity-building* to a lifelong and for all practical purposes unfinishable process of *identification*. Perhaps the most important modification is the fading of the monopolistic ambitions of the 'entity of belonging'.

As signalled above, the referents of 'belonging', unlike in orthodox 'integrative communities', have no tools to monitor the strength of the dedication of 'members': neither are they interested in demanding and promoting the members' unswerving loyalty and undivided allegiance. In its contemporary liquid modern rendition, 'belonging' to one entity may be joined by and shared with belonging to other entities in almost any combination, without necessarily arousing condemnation and provoking repressive measures from any of them. Attachments tend to lose much of their past intensity, since as a rule much of their vehemence and vigour, just like the partisan spirit of those 'attached', is tempered by other, simultaneous allegiances. Hardly any kind of 'belonging' these days engages 'the whole self', since each person at any moment of their life is involved in, so to speak, 'multiple belongings'. Being only partly loyal, or loyal so to speak 'à la carte', is no longer necessarily viewed as tantamount to disloyalty, let alone betrayal.

Hence the present-day recasting of the phenomenon of (cultural) 'hybridity' (combining traits specific to, and derived from, different and separate species): from something frowned upon or explicitly condemned as a token of *déclassement*, into a virtue and a sign of distinction. In the emergent scales of cultural superiority and social prestige, 'hybrids' (whether 'genuine' or self-proclaimed) tend to occupy the top ranks, and the manifestation of 'hybridity' becomes a widely favoured tool of upward sociocultural mobility. Being self-confined or condemned in perpetuity to one self-enclosed set of values and behavioural patterns, on the other hand, is increasingly viewed as a sign of sociocultural inferiority or deprivation. 'Integrative communities' are now to be found mostly, perhaps even exclusively, at the lower rungs of the sociocultural ladder.

For the art of life, this new setting opens unprecedented vistas. Freedom of self-creation has never before achieved such a breathtaking scope, simultaneously exciting and frightening. Never before has the need for orientation points and helpful guides been as strong or as painfully felt. Yet never before have firm and reliable orientation points and trustworthy guides been in such short supply (at least short in relation to the volume and intensity of need).

Let us be clear: there is a vexing shortage of *firm and reliable* orientation points and *trustworthy* guides. That shortage (paradoxically, yet not at all accidentally) coincides with an unprecedented proliferation of tempting suggestions and seductive offers of orientation, with a constantly rising wave of guidebooks and swelling throngs of counsellors – making it, however, a yet more confusing task to cut through the thicket of misleading or downright deceitful propositions in order to find an orientation likely to deliver on its promise . . .

Nicolas Sarkozy, the newly elected president of France, declared in a television interview in June 2007: 'I am not a theoretician. I am not an ideologue. Oh, I am not an intellectual! I am someone concrete!'[17] What possibly could he mean by saying that?

Most certainly, he did not mean that unlike the 'ideologues' he does not hold unswervingly to certain beliefs, while equally resolutely rejecting others. He is, after all, on record as a man with strong views, firmly believing 'in doing rather than musing', and calling on the French during his presidential campaign 'to work more and earn more'. He told the electors repeatedly that it is good to work harder and longer hours in order to get rich (a call which the French seem to have found attractive, yet were far from unanimous in believing to be pragmatically sound: according to a TBS-Sofres poll, by contrast with 40 per cent who believe that one can get rich through working, 39 per cent of the French believe that it is possible to get rich by winning the lottery). Such declarations, as long as they are sincere, meet all the conditions of an ideology and perform the major function which ideologies are expected to perform: they instruct people what to do and reassure them that doing it will bring beneficial results. They also manifest an agonistic, partisan stance towards alternative convictions: a feature normally taken as a trademark of ideologies.

Only one feature of 'ideologies as we have known them thus far' is perhaps missing from Nicolas Sarkozy's life philosophy: a vision of a 'social totality' that, as Émile Durkheim suggested, is 'greater than the sum of its parts', that (unlike, say, a sack of potatoes) is *not* reducible to the sum total of the separate units it contains; a *social* totality that cannot be reduced to an aggregate of *individuals* pursuing their own private aims and guided by their own private desires and rules. The repeated public statements of the French president suggest, on the contrary, just such a reduction.

It does not seem that the predictions of the 'end of ideology', rife and widely accepted up to around twenty years ago, have come true or are about to. What we are witnessing is, rather, a curious twist currently happening to the idea of 'ideology'. In defiance of a long tradition, the ideology currently advocated from on high for popular use is a belief that thinking about a 'totality' and composing visions of a 'good society' are a waste of time, since they are irrelevant to individual happiness and a successful life.

The ideology of the new type is not a *privatized ideology*. Such a notion would be an oxymoron, since a supply of security and self-confidence, which is the *tour de force* of ideologies and the prime condition of their seductiveness, would be unattainable without massive *public* endorsement. This is rather an *ideology of privatization*. The call to 'work more and earn more', a call addressed to individuals and fit only for individual use, is chasing away and replacing the calls of the past to 'think of society' and 'care for society' (for a community, a nation, a church, a cause). Sarkozy is not the first to try to trigger or accelerate that shift; that priority belongs rather to Margaret Thatcher's memorable announcement that 'There is no such thing as Society. There are individual men and women and there are families.'

This is a new ideology for the new *individualized society*, of which Ulrich Beck has written that individual men and women are now expected, pushed and pulled to seek and find individual solutions to socially created problems and implement those solutions individually using individual skills and resources. This ideology proclaims the futility (indeed, counterproductivity) of solidarity: of joining forces and subordinating individual actions to a 'common cause'. It derides the principle of communal responsibility for the well-being of its members, decrying it as a recipe for a debilitating 'nanny state', and warning against care for the other leading to an abhorrent and detestable 'dependency'.

This is also an ideology made to the measure of the new *society of consumers*. It represents the world as a warehouse of potential objects of consumption, individual life as a perpetual search for bargains, its purpose as maximal consumer satisfaction, and life success as an increase in the individual's own market value. Widely accepted and firmly embraced, it dismisses competing life philosophies with a curt 'TINA' ('There is no alternative'). Having degraded and silenced its competitors, it becomes, in Pierre Bourdieu's memorable expression, veritably *la pensée unique*.

Not for nothing are the remarkably popular 'Big Brother' shows presented as *'reality* TV'. That denomination suggests that off-screen life, 'the real thing', is like the on-screen saga of 'Big Brother' competitors. Here as there, no one playing the game of survival is guaranteed to survive, permission to stay in the game is just a temporary reprieve, and team loyalty is only 'until further notice' – that is, it won't outlive its usefulness in promoting individual interest. That *someone* will be excluded is beyond dispute; the only question is *who* it will be, and hence what is at issue is not the *abolishing* of exclusions (a task that would favour joining forces and solidarity of action) but *shifting the threat of exclusion away from oneself and towards the others* (a task that prompts self-concern while rendering solidarity unreasonable, if not suicidal). In the 'Big Brother' show, someone *must* be excluded each week: not because, by some curious coincidence, regularly, every week, one person is found to be inadequate, but because exclusion has been written into the rules of 'reality' as seen on TV. Exclusion is in the nature of things, an undetachable aspect of being-in-the-world, a 'law of nature', so to speak – and so to rebel against it makes no sense. The only issue worthy of being thought about, and intensely, is how to stave off the prospect of being the one to be excluded in the next week's round of exclusions.

At least in the affluent part of the planet, the stake of cut-throat individual competition is no longer physical survival – or the satisfaction of the primary biological needs demanded by the survival instinct. Neither is it the right to self-assert, to set one's own objectives and to decide what kind of life one would prefer to live; to exercise such rights is, on the contrary, assumed to be every individual's duty. It is, moreover, assumed that whatever happens to the individual is the consequence either of exercising such rights, or of an abominable failure or sinful refusal to exercise them. And so whatever happens to the individual will be retrospectively interpreted as another confirmation of the individuals' sole and inalienable responsibility for their individual plight – adversity as much as success.

Once cast as individuals, we are encouraged to actively seek 'social recognition' for what have been preinterpreted as our individual choices: namely, for the forms of life which we, the individuals, are practising (whether by choice or by default). 'Social recognition' means acceptance that the individual who practises that form of life leads a worthy and decent life and on this ground deserves the respect owed and offered to other worthy and decent people.

The alternative to social recognition is denial of dignity: humiliation. In Dennis Smith's recent definition, 'the act is humiliating if it forcefully overrides or contradicts the claim that particular individuals . . . are making about who they are and where and how they fit in';[18] in other words, if individuals are, explicitly or implicitly, denied the recognition which they expected for the person they are and/or the kind of life they live; and if they are refused the entitlements that would have been made available or have continued to be available following such recognition. A person feels humiliated when she or he is 'brutally shown, by words, actions or events, that they cannot be what they think they are . . . Humiliation is the experience of being unfairly, unreasonably and unwillingly pushed down, held down, held back or pushed out.'[19]

That feeling breeds resentment. In a society of individuals like ours, this is arguably the most venomous and implacable variety of resentment a person may feel and the most common and prolific cause of conflict, dissent, rebellion and thirst for revenge. Denial of recognition, refusal of respect and the threat of exclusion have replaced exploitation and discrimination as the formulae most commonly used to explain and justify the grudges individuals might feel towards society, or to the sections or aspects of society to which they are directly exposed (personally or through the media) and which they experience first-hand.

This does not mean that humiliation is a novel phenomenon specific to the present stage in the history of modern society. On the contrary, it is as old as human sociability and togetherness. It means, however, that in the individualized society of consumers the most common and 'most telling' definitions and explanations of the resulting pain and grievance have presently moved, or are moving, away from group- or category-related features and towards *personal* referents. And rather than being ascribed to injustice or a malfunctioning of the social whole, so that a remedy can be sought in the reform of *society*, individual suffering tends increasingly to be perceived as the outcome of a personal offence and an assault on personal dignity and self-esteem, calling for a *personal* response or a personal revenge.

As individuals are called on to invent and deploy individual solutions to socially produced discomforts, they tend to respond in kind. What they respond to is a turn of events that plays havoc with the expectations suggested by a person-focused ideology. That turn of events is perceived and 'made sense of' by the same ideology of privatization as a *personal* snub, a personally aimed (even if randomly targeted) humiliation; its first casualties are self-respect and the sentiments of security and self-confidence. The affected individuals feel debased, and since the ideology of privatization assumes the presence of a culprit behind every case of suffering or discomfort, the feeling of being debased rebounds as a feverish search for the persons guilty of doing the debasing; the conflict and enmity, just like the harm of which they stand accused, are deemed *personal*. The guilty ones must be located, exposed, publicly condemned and punished. The 'them' nominated by the ideology of privatization are as individualized as are those whom that ideology designates as 'us'.

As has already been suggested, the ideology under discussion is wrapped around the issue of identity. Who am I? What is my place among the others – among the ones I know, the ones I know of, or perhaps the ones I have so far never heard of? What are the threats that make this place of mine insecure? Who stands behind those threats? What kinds of countermeasures should I undertake in order to disable those people and so stave off such threats? This is how the questions which ideologies were (and still are) believed to answer in a resolute and authoritative manner are being rephrased for the use of the members of individualized society.

This new ideology is as conservative as Mannheim believed ideologies (as opposed to utopias) to be. It raises the daily experiences of the world we currently inhabit to be the indomitable laws of the universe, and the viewpoint of individuals-by-decree to be the only perspective from which the state of the world can be ascertained. Those among us who, thanks to their resourcefulness and skills, feel like fish in the water in that world may not note the yawning gap stretching between the expectations the ideology of privatization aims to arouse in *all* individuals-by-decree, and the realistic chances of scores of men and women who lack the resources and the skills without which the rise of individuals-de-jure to the status of individuals-de-facto is unthinkable. Those *failed* individuals – individuals doomed to suffer the humiliation of inadequacy and of falling below standards that others evidently have no difficulty in meeting, and the humiliation of being charged with and vilified for sloth and indolence, if not for an inborn inferiority – will not fail to note the gap, however, when they fall into it and fathom its abysmal depth, as sooner or later they must.

This ideology, like all other known ideologies, *divides* humanity. But in addition it also divides its own believers, enabling some and disabling the rest. By so doing, it exacerbates the conflict-ridden character of the individualized/privatized society. Through defusing the energies and disabling the forces that could potentially undercut its foundations, this ideology also conserves that society and dims the prospects of its overhaul.

3

The Choice

The energy released by the desire for happiness may take the form of either centripetal or centrifugal force. 'Centrifugal', according to the definition of the Oxford English Dictionary, means 'flying or tending to fly *off* from the centre'. 'Centripetal' is the opposite of 'centrifugal': it means 'tending *towards* the centre'. The 'centre' to which both definitions refer, the centre where the force originates and from which it emanates – from which its centrifugal variety 'flies off' and to which its centripetal companion/alternative falls back – is the *happiness-desiring subject*. And this means *each one of us*, as long as we all consider the pursuit of happiness to be our challenge and task and make the pursuit of happiness our life strategy.

To put the alternatives we all confront simply, in a nutshell as it were: my pursuit of happiness may focus on care for *my own* well-being, or on care for the well-being of *others*. Russell Jacoby has telescoped the choice involved in summarizing his experience with successive generations of students: 'Once students dreamed of healing the ills of society; now – based on the students I have – they dream of going to good law schools.'[1]

The two alternatives are not necessarily in contradiction; they may operate simultaneously, with little or no conflict or clash. However, while the *centripetal* force may, so to speak, 'go it alone', and for it to act in the company of its alternative, the centrifugal force, is not a necessary requirement, the *centrifugal* force must have a simultaneously centripetal effect. Caring for the well-being of an-Other, 'being good' for an-Other, also enhances the 'feel-good' feeling and so presumably the happiness of the caring subject. In that case, the opposition between selfishness and altruism melts and vanishes. The two attitudes appear to stand in stark, unreconcilable opposition to each other only when contemplated from the perspective of the centripetal force.

Indeed, then – and only then – will questions like 'Why should I be good to him (or her)?', 'What is in it for me?', 'What has he (or she) done for me to justify my care?' arise. And only then will the calculation start of gains and losses, input–output ratios, costs and effects. Only then would one be tempted to ask, 'Will my profits compensate for my sacrifices?' From the perspective of centripetal preoccupations, the wisdom and benefits of the cen-trifugal impetus are cast in doubt; perhaps even derogated, dis-missed and condemned as counterproductive.

Ethical philosophers have tried hard to make a bridge between the two shores of the river of life: *self*-interest, and care for *others*. As is their habit, the philosophers struggled to muster and articu-late convincing arguments that were able, or at least hoped, to resolve the apparent contradiction and settle the controversy beyond reasonable doubt – once and for all. The philosophers tried to demonstrate that obedience to moral commandments is in the 'self-interest' of the obedient; that costs of being moral will be repaid with profits; that others will repay kindness to them in the same currency; that caring for others and being good to others is, in short, a valuable, perhaps even indispensable, part of a per-son's self-care. Some arguments were more ingenious than others, some were backed with more authority and so carried more per-suasion, but all circled around the quasi-empirical, yet empirically untested assumption that 'if you are good to others, others will be good to you'.

Despite all the efforts, however, the empirical evidence was hard to come by – or, if anything, remained ambiguous. The assumption did not square well with the personal experiences of too many people, who found all too often that it was the selfish, insensitive and cynical people who gathered all the prizes, while the tender and big-hearted, compassionate people ready to sacri-fice their own peace and comfort for the sake of others found themselves, time and again, duped, spurned and pitied, or ridiculed for their credulity and unwarranted (since unreciprocated) trust. It was never too difficult to collect ample proof for the suspicion that most gains tend to go to the self-concerned, while those concerned with the welfare of others are more often than not left to count their losses. Today particularly, collecting such evidence perhaps gets easier by the day. As Lawrence Grossberg puts it, 'it is increasingly difficult to locate places where it is possible to care about something enough, to have enough faith that it matters, so that one can actually make a commitment to it and invest oneself in it.'[2] Grossberg coins the name 'ironic nihilism' for the attitude of people who, if pressed, might have reported the reasoning behind their motives in the following way:

I know cheating is wrong and I know I am cheating, but that is the way things are, that is what reality is like. One knows that life, and every choice, is a scam, but the knowledge has become so universally accepted that there are no longer any alternatives. Everyone knows everyone cheats, so everyone cheats, and if I did not, I would in effect suffer for being honest.

Other reservations, yet more salient, have however been voiced against the philosophers' assumption. For instance: if you decide to be kind to others *because* you expect a reward for your kindness, if the hoped-for *reward* is the motive of your good deeds, if 'being kind and good to others' is a result of calculating your probable gains and losses, then is your way of acting really a manifestation of a *moral* stance, or rather one more case of mercenary, selfish behaviour? And a yet more profound, truly radical doubt: can goodness be a matter of argument, persuasion, 'talking over', 'bringing round', deciding that 'it stands to reason'? Is goodness to others an outcome of a *rational* decision, and could it therefore be prompted by an appeal to reason? Can goodness be *taught*? Arguments supporting both the positive and the negative answers to such questions have been advanced, but so far none commands uncontested authority. The jury is still out . . .

In her milestone study *When Light Pierced the Darkness*, Nechama Tec reported the results of her research intended to locate the factors that determined, or at least inclined, some of the witnesses of the destruction of Polish Jews to save lives of the

victims while risking their own.[3] In Poland, unlike in most of the
Nazi-occupied countries of Europe, death was the statutory punishment for the crime of helping Jews to hide – or even for failing
to report to the police any neighbours guilty of such a crime.
Many people defied the Nazis and their willing helpers and preferred to risk their own lives than to idly watch the unspeakable
atrocities perpetrated on men, women and children accused of
belonging to the 'wrong race'. As one would expect of an impec-
cably trained and seasoned sociologist, Tec calculated the correla-
tions between willingness to help and readiness for self-sacrifice,
and all the factors commonly presumed to determine human
behaviour: factors believed to shape individual attitudes, values,
life philosophy and the probability of preferring one kind of
behaviour over another – such factors as class, wealth, education,
religious beliefs and political allegiance. To her surprise and that
of her fellow sociologists, she found no correlation. There was, it
appeared, no 'statistically significant' factor determining moral
behaviour. As far as the accumulated wisdom of sociology could
opine, the helpers did not differ from the rest of the Polish popula-
tion, even if the moral value of their conduct and the human significance of its consequences differed most radically from the
responses of the majority. In the face of human choices between
good and evil, sociological wisdom was found to have nothing
to say . . .

To social scientists, as Amos Oz caustically commented in his
Goethe Prize acceptance speech on 28 August 2005,

> all human motives and actions derive from circumstances, which
> are often beyond personal control . . . We are controlled by our
> social background. For about a hundred years now, they have been
> telling us that we are motivated exclusively by economic self-inter-
> est, that we are mere products of our ethnic cultures, that we are
> no more than marionettes of our own subconscious.

Oz disagreed:

> Personally I believe that every human being, in his or her own
> hearts, is capable of telling good from bad . . . It may sometimes
> be hard to define good, but evil has its unmistakable odour: every
> child knows what pain is. Therefore, each time we deliberately

inflict pain on another, we know what we are doing. We are doing evil.[4]

For once, the sociologists – self-proclaimed masters of foolproof or nearly foolproof research methods – are obliged to bow to the opinion of a widely acclaimed master of insight, vision and empathy. Obliged indeed, since when it comes to moral selves and ethical judgement, inventories of determinants and statistics of their distribution are of little use.

So why did the helpers risk joining the ranks of the victims, rather than lock their doors and shut their blinds to avoid the sight of their suffering? The only answer to pass the test of the evidence from the history of the Holocaust is that the helpers, unlike many or most other people of the same social category, education, religious faith and political loyalties, *could not do otherwise*. They would not be able to go on living if they failed to defend the lives of others. Protecting their own physical safety and comfort could not make up for the spiritual distress caused by the sight of people who were suffering. Probably, they would never have been able to forgive themselves if they had put their own welfare above the welfare of those whom they could have saved.

To obtain forgiveness from others would probably have been easier than to placate their own consciences. In the draconic law of October 1942 which introduced capital punishment for 'Jew-helpers', those appalled by the sight of inhumanity might have, like so many others, found a (convincing!) excuse for desisting from action: 'I sincerely wished I could have done something to help, but I *could not* – I would have been killed or sent to a concentration camp if I had.' Saying that, they would appeal to the 'good sense' of the majority of their listeners – but they would also pre-empt rather than resolve the moral quandary by trying to plug their ears against the voice of their conscience. To say that, they would have to have already decided that their lives were more worthy of care than the lives of those others for whose survival they refused to care, while counting on being reassured and reinforced in their conviction of their own righteousness by the explicit or at least tacit approval of their choice by the myriads of similarly self-concerned individuals. The voice of conscience, however, while it might have been refused a hearing, wouldn't be silenced.

In a debate on Polish–Jewish relations under the Nazi occupation, conducted on Professor Jan Błoński's initiative in the pages of the Polish weekly *Tygodnik Powszechny* in 1987, Jerzy Jastrzębowski recalled a story told by an older member of his family. The family offered to hide an old friend, a Jew who looked like a Polish Gentile and spoke the refined kind of Polish to be expected of someone born in a nest of Polish gentlefolk – but declined to do the same for his three sisters, who looked Jewish and spoke with a pronounced Yiddish inflection. Their friend, however, refused to be saved alone. Jastrzębowski comments:

> Had the decision of my family been different, there were nine chances to one that we would all be shot. The probability that our friend and his sisters would survive in those conditions was perhaps smaller still. And yet the person telling me this family drama and repeating 'what could we do, there was nothing we could do', did not look me in the eyes. He sensed I felt a lie, though all the facts were true.

In the Russian film *Vremia Biedy* (roughly 'Troubled times') an old peasant woman, a helpless witness to the atrocities of forced collectivization and then again to the Nazi occupation, and unable to take in more of the same, sets herself on fire. From her burning hut her last words can be heard: 'Forgive me, all of you whom I *could not* help!' In an apocryphal Talmudic story, a saintly sage walking with a donkey loaded with sacks full of food comes across a beggar who asks him for something to eat. The kind-hearted man promptly, and in a great hurry, starts to untie the sacks, but before he manages to reach the food, prolonged hunger takes its toll and the beggar dies. The sage, in despair, falls on his knees and prays to God to punish him for 'failing to save the life of my fellow man'.

Both the stories above might surely strike the reader as 'excessive' in the standards they imply, or illogical (even 'unjust', in so far as justice is supposed to be meted out in accordance with the logic of causality). Both self-proclaimed culprits would surely be exonerated in any ordinary court of law, were they to be charged for what they believed was their guilt. But morality has its own logic, and in the court of conscience the heroes of the stories stand little chance.

Why people respond so differently to apparently identical situations was and remains a mystery which old and new theologians, philosophers, and innumerable professionals of the human and natural sciences, as well as the theorists and practitioners of education, have attempted and continue to try to crack – in vain. Despite disappointing results (or perhaps because of them), the attempts are unlikely to be abandoned. The motives for continuing them may vary, yet each one is overwhelming and impossible to resist. Theologians need to comprehend what is admittedly incomprehensible: the wisdom of God's creation and of the divine administration of human affairs, which (if penetrated . . .) would reveal and reconfirm the presumed link, difficult as it is to prove, between divine grace, obedience to the commandments, piety and virtue, and the happy life, and that other link between the sinful life and a life of misery (this-worldly or other-worldly). Philosophers cannot and will not bear phenomena that elude explanation and defy argument; they will not rest until a logic is found that will debunk them as figments of the imagination, or at least make sense of their obstinate presence. Scientists, in full agreement with the technologists, their executive arm and increasingly a prime source of stimulation, want to know the laws that determine the shape and the conduct of things animate as much as inanimate, hoping that to know them will mean to control the shape and the conduct of things, and that to know them fully will eventually come to mean controlling them completely. And the educators, obviously, dream of pupils who are like a well-tempered clavier, so that pressing any keys will regularly produce the sounds dictated by the score, with never a discordant note.

Francis Fukuyama (of 'end of history' notoriety) suggested recently that the totalitarian dreams inspired by the Enlightenment and persistent since then of producing 'new humans' made to the measure of the genuine potential of human beings (that is, up to the standard adumbrated in the designers' blueprints) were neither ill-conceived nor unrealistic; those dreams, Fukuyama insists, have failed solely for having been dreamed before their time, under conditions not yet ready for their realization. Concentration camps, brainwashing and reflex conditioning were wrong means to the right ends: ineffective, shamefully primitive and pitifully inadequate to the task. On the other hand, present-day advances in neurosurgery, biochemistry and genetic engineering have finally lifted the available means to the level of the task still waiting to be performed. At long last, we have arrived at the threshold of a new era of *new humans* ...

Whether Fukuyama is right this time may be, to say the least, a moot question; what is not in doubt, however, is the connection between the new feats of technoscience and the advent of an era of new fears and new dystopias. Fears and dystopias have surely risen to the level of the new prospects made feasible by the new technoscience. Orwell's *1984* and Huxley's *Brave New World*, now outdated, have been elbowed out by Houellebecq's *Possibility of an Island*.

Both the utopias and the dystopias specialize in adumbrating the predetermined destination of current developments: utopias present the land at the end of the road as a site of harmony and order, a destination to be looked forward to and if possible to be brought nearer; whereas dystopias portray that land as at best an open-air prison, something to be feared, kept as far away as possible, and ideally made forever off-limits. Such radically opposed visions notwithstanding, they both pretend that there is a finishing line to the running track of history, and that this line can be drawn or anticipated in advance; this pretence is probably the main reason for the two mental products of the modern mind to be listed in thesauruses in the unflattering company of castles in the air, pipe dreams (or nightmares), chimeras, flights of fancy and illusions. Whether armed initially with the 'eu' prefix (denoting something good) or the 'dys' prefix (signalling something bad), both visions end up with the prefix 'ou', meaning nowhere ...

It looks as if there is no preordained final destination, no predetermined finishing line to the roads along which we move, including the road allegedly leading to 'new humans' – however authoritative or even foolproof their computer-supported models may appear, cleansed of all human indetermination, unpredictability, and (yes!) free will and free choice. However long the scientifically composed inventory of determinants, and however profuse the technical tools available to manage them, humans remain stubbornly addicted to choices that play havoc with extant rules and routines, and are therefore notorious for their habit of defying prediction, for the randomness and irregularity of their conduct, for inconstancy, vagaries and levity, and altogether for what any manager worth her or his salt would describe, outraged, as the sin of *undependability*. One quality with which humans are blessed or cursed, and which they are unlikely ever to forfeit or allow to be taken away or suppressed, is free will . . .

Caprices are the trademark of the world 'out there' – not only of human beings, cast into it and trying to cut their way through the thicket of chance as well as being pressed (and expected) to discover that way and to follow it resolutely. Those caprices, irritatingly insensitive and indifferent to human plans and predictions, are commonly reported under the name of 'accidents'. In a film under just that title, Krzysztof Kieślowski tells the story of three alternative lives that might have been lived by the same young man, each life starting from the hero's attempt to jump into a train already leaving the station. In one story, the hero manages to catch the train. In another, he misses it. In yet another, he runs after it, trying to catch the speeding train beyond the end of the passengers' platform, where he is promptly stopped by an armed guard, taken to a police station, arrested and charged with trespassing.

The only feature shared by the lives that follow the three different 'accidents' is the person of the hero. The three lives are lived in totally different social settings subject to drastically differing norms, and among totally different people pursuing totally different objectives with totally different means. A trained sociologist, in full agreement with common and seldom questioned wisdom, would retrospectively classify each life in a social category different from the others in virtually every respect – politically, culturally, and morally. One is the trajectory of a politically indifferent specialist, a doctor fully engrossed in tending to his patients while unconcerned with anything in that wide world outside the hospital walls except for matters bearing on his professional and job-related interests. The other is the career of a militant political activist, wholly dedicated to fulfilling the tasks as spelled out by the party bosses. The third is the martyrdom of a hard-boiled dissident and underground fighter. In a fraction of a second, three completely different life itineraries of a young man trying to catch a moving train have branched off the common stem – never to cross again.

Richard Rorty objects to the suggestion by Christopher Hitchens that George Orwell's political biography reflected only one factor: his character – his honesty and intelligence – which made him make the right choices under any circumstances; that is, the kinds of choices of which Hitchens, in unison with the prevailing opinion of the next century, would approve.[5] Suppose, says Rorty, Orwell had taken 'a different route into Spain, had fought on another front, had never served in a POUM unit, had accepted the Stalinist version of what happened in the streets of Barcelona, and so had never had occasion to write *Homage to Catalonia*. He might then, after World War II, have opposed Churchill's anti-Communism as fiercely as he did his pro-colonialism.'

As the meteorologist Edward Lorenz found to his utter amazement, a butterfly flapping its wings in Beijing on a spring day could well change the trajectories of the autumn hurricanes in the Gulf of Mexico. So what? Is human life ruled by accidents? Accidents that cannot be anticipated – let alone averted, rolled back, revoked, made null and void? Does it matter what we choose? In short – in shaping our lives, are we the cues, the cue-holders, or the billiard balls? Are we players, or are we played?

The principal protagonists of Florian Henckel von Donnersmarck's film *The Life of Others* are crowded together in the same tiny corner of a totalitarian country where no nook or cranny is not under surveillance, and any free choice, just because it is freely made, is viewed as a crime against the state and treated accordingly. Artists of the theatre – playwrights, directors and actors, people who by the logic of their vocation embody the idea of imagination, ingenuity, originality and free choice – populate that corner. They are not alone, though. Even in their most intimate and private moments they have company: Big Brother is never asleep, Big Brother's eyes are always watching, Big Brother's ears always listening. Free (fitful, frivolous) moves in Big Brother's game of grace and disgrace, favours and disfavours, reach the studios, stages and bedrooms of the artists in the guise of accidents . . . There are too many such 'accidents' for those on the receiving side to cope, let alone to fight back against their effects. A tight spot, indeed, and a spot they all share: the meek and the bold, the careerists and the fighters alike. Shuffled and reshuffled between secret police files, the artists have little choice but to behave as billiard balls do, go where they are pushed and follow the ways preordained for the category to which they have been assigned – and bear the consequences. Or do they?

All the major protagonists of von Donnersmarck's film may share the same tight spot, but here the similarities between them end. One, a blacklisted director, has first of all chosen a clear conscience and loyalty to his artistic vision, and then suicide, over the price he would need to pay in the currency of dishonesty and betrayal for access to tools of trade and permission to create. Another, the playwright, the Big Brother's favourite showpiece intellectual, has chosen permission to be published and performed, applauded, written about and showered with state prizes, over the bliss of telling the truth, the whole truth and nothing but the truth. The third, a universally adored and idolized actress, was ready to sell her body and to report on fellow actors rather than suffer a ban on stage appearances; threatened with being refiled as 'in disgrace', she betrays to the inquisitors the hiding place of the typewriter on which a pamphlet critical of the tyrannical state was typed, and which, if found, could serve as evidence in a show trial and condemn the playwright – the man whom she loves and by whom she is loved – to oblivion. But it is her inquisitor, known to be a pastmaster of pitiless interrogation, who out of compassion for the love that is about to be destroyed secretly removes the incriminating evidence and staves off disaster. The blacklisted director bequeaths his never staged *Sonata for a Good Man* to his friend, the playwright, as a farewell gift – just before committing suicide. After the fall of the Stasi-supported regime, the playwright dedicates his new play under the same title to the man who, in his inquisitorial past, chose humanity over obedience and career.

All artists struggle with the resistance of the material on which they wish to engrave their visions. All works of art bear the traces of that struggle – of its victories, defeats, and the many enforced, though not less shameful for that reason, compromises. Artists of life and their works are no exception to that rule. The chisels used by the artists of life (knowingly or not, and with greater or lesser skill) in their engraving efforts are their *characters*. Thomas Hardy referred to that principle when declaring that 'the fate of man is his character'. *Fate* and its guerrilla troops, accidents, decide the sets of choices confronting the artists of life. But it is *character* that decides which choices are made.

Settings make some choices more probable than others. Character defies those probabilities. It deprives the accidents, including their genuine, putative or suspected manipulators behind the scenes, of the omnipotence they are believed or claim to possess. Between resigned acceptance and the bold decision to defy the force of circumstances stands character. It is the actor's character that submits the choices which have triumphantly passed the test of *probability* to the other, much more demanding test of *acceptability*. It was his character that impelled Martin Luther on 31 October 1517, the eve of All Saints', to declare '*Ich* kann nicht anders' when affixing his ninety-five heretical theses to the church door of the Wittenberg castle.

In the view of Knud Løgstrup, one of the most acute ethical philosophers of the past century, the hope of morality (that is, of care for the Other; or more demandingly, but closer still to the essence of morality, *being for* the Other) is vested in its *prereflexive spontaneity*: 'Mercy is spontaneous because the least interruption, the least calculation, the least dilution of it in order to serve something else destroys it entirely, indeed turns it into the opposite of what it is, unmercifulness.'[6] Emmanuel Levinas, another great ethical philosopher of the last century, is known to insist that the question 'Why should I be moral?' (that is, asking for arguments of the kind 'Is there something in it for me?', 'What did she or he do for me to justify my care?', 'Why should I care if so many others don't?', or 'Why could not someone else do it instead of me?') is not the *starting point* of moral conduct, but a signal of its imminent collapse and *decease*. All amorality, in Levinas's view, began with Cain's question 'Am I my brother's keeper?', demanding 'proof' that caring for his brother was indeed his duty; and assuming that caring might become a duty only at the behest of a superior power, presumably armed with sanctions to punish the disobedient. Løgstrup, with his reliance on spontaneity, the impulse and the urge to trust others rather than the inclination to calculate one's own gains and losses, would surely have agreed with Levinas's verdict.

Both philosophers seem to concede that the *need* for morality, or just the *advisability* of morality, cannot and does not need to be discursively established, let alone proved; and that, moreover, the very expression 'need for morality' ought to be rejected as an oxymoron – since whatever answers a 'need' is something other than morality. They share the opinion that conduct undertaken with a view to other people's good is not moral if it is not disinterested: an act is moral in as far as it is an uncalculated, natural, spontaneous and mostly unreflected-upon manifestation of humanity. (Objecting to Stephen Toulmin's suggestion that an act is 'moral' when it agrees with a 'general principle'[7] and referring to the most often quoted example chosen by Toulmin to illustrate his thesis, Løgstrup insisted that 'if the motivating reason for my returning the [borrowed] book to John at the promised time is not one of consideration for John but my resolve to live in accordance with the general principle that promises should be kept, my act is not moral but moralistic.'[8]) A moral act does not 'serve' any 'purpose' and most surely is not guided by the expectation of profit, comfort, notoriety, ego-boosting, public applause or any other kind of self-promotion. Though it is true that 'objectively good' – helpful and useful – deeds have been performed time and again out of the actor's calculation of gain – be it the earning of Divine grace, the purchasing of public esteem, or repentance to earn absolution from sin and Divine forgiveness for unfeeling acts or heartlessness on other occasions – they could not be classified as genuinely *moral* acts precisely because they were so *motivated*.

In moral acts, any 'ulterior motive is ruled out', Løgstrup insists. The spontaneous expression of life is *radical* thanks precisely to 'the absence of ulterior motives' – including, and perhaps including first of all, the absence of motives of gain or the avoidance of punishment. This is one crucial reason why the ethical demand, that 'objective' pressure to be moral emanating from the very fact of being alive and sharing the planet with other living beings, is and must stay *silent*. Obedience to the ethical demand along the lines of following an order because of the fear of the punitive sanctions which would befall the disobedient would not be the moral act intended by the ethical demand. Conformity is *not* morality, even if it is in response to an order to do some specific good. There is no 'must' in morality – no command, no coercion; moral acts are intrinsically *free choices*, expressions of the self's freedom to act (unfree human beings – were such a contradiction in terms plausible – would not be 'moral beings'). Paradoxically (or not at all paradoxically), to follow the ethical demand means to forget its coercive power. To follow the ethical demand means to be guided solely by the good of the Other.

The immediacy of human contact is sustained by the immediate expressions of life; it needs, indeed tolerates, no other support. The ethical demand is taciturn, it does not spell out what form the care for others should take. But its power consists precisely in its reticence and taciturnity, thanks to which it stops short of giving orders, threatening sanctions and reducing the moral act to another case of conformity to the powers on high. This time, it is Levinas who would have wholeheartedly agreed with Løgstrup. Levinas kept repeating that the Other commands us to care by his *weakness*, not by his *power*; in other words, by his *inability* and/or *unwillingness* to give us orders and compel us to perform what has been ordered. We are not compelled to take a moral stance by a superior power. It is ultimately up to us, and us alone, to submit to the challenge of the Face of the Other and decide how to give content to the shock of our responsibility for an-Other. As Richard A. Cohen, the translator of Levinas's conversation with Philippe Nemo, summed it up: 'ethical exigency is not an ontological necessity. The prohibition against killing does not render murder impossible. It renders it evil.' The 'being' of ethics consists solely in 'disturbing the complacency of being'.[9]

In practical terms, this means that however humans may resent being left alone to their own counsel and own responsibility, it is precisely that loneliness that contains a hope of a morally impregnated togetherness. A *hope* not a *certainty*, let alone a *guaranteed* certainty. Not even a high probability, that dreamed-of and sought-after assurance warranted by the evidence of statistical trends . . .

The spontaneity and sovereignty of life expressions do not vouch for the resulting conduct being an ethically proper, laudable choice between good and evil. Both wrong *and* right choices arise from the same condition of uncertainty, underdetermination, underdefinition and the dearth of coercion – as does the impulse to run cravenly for cover obligingly provided by the authoritative commands of an absolution-granting power armed with sanctions, *and* as does the boldness to accept personal responsibility for a decision to act taken despite the temptation to shift it to other agencies, particularly agencies equipped with superior powers. Without bracing oneself for the possibility of wrong choices, one is unlikely to persevere in the search for the right choice. Far from being a major threat to morality (it is viewed as a vexing abomination by many an ethical philosopher!), *uncertainty is the home ground of the moral person and the only soil in which morality can sprout and flourish.*

Under the present-day regime of deregulation and privatization, the promise and the practice of 'relief from responsibility' have remained much the same as they were in the earlier stages of modern history: now as then, they resort to the injection of a measure of genuine or putative clarity into a hopelessly opaque situation – and they do it through replacing (more correctly, covering up) the mind-boggling complexity of the task with a set of straightforward 'must do' and 'mustn't do' rules. Now as then, individual actors are pressed, nudged and/or cajoled to put their trust in authorities to decide and spell out what exactly the unspoken demand commands them to do in this or that situation, and just how far (and no further) their unconditional responsibility then obliges them to go. The stratagem remains much the same, but nowadays different tools tend to be deployed in its service.

The concepts of responsibility and responsible choice, which resided before in the semantic field of the ethical duty to care for the needs of the Other, have now moved or been shifted to the realm of self-fulfilment and the calculation of a person's own risks; it has been put in the service of centripetal, self-referential concerns. In the process, 'the Other' as the trigger, the target and the yardstick of a responsibility accepted, assumed and acted upon has all but disappeared from view, elbowed out or overshadowed by the actor's own self. 'Responsibility' means now, first and last, *responsibility to oneself* ('you deserve this', 'you owe this to yourself', as the outspoken traders in 'relief from responsibility' nowadays tend to repeat), while 'responsible choices' are, first and last, those moves which will serve the interests and satisfy the desires of the actor and stave off the need to compromise while precluding self-sacrifice.

The outcome is not much different from the 'adiaphorizing'[10] effects of the stratagem practised by bureaucracy in the 'solid' phase of the modern era. That stratagem consisted of the substitution of 'responsibility *to*' (a superior person, an authority, a 'noble cause' and its spokesmen originating the action) for 'responsibility *for*' (the welfare, autonomy and dignity of another human being placed at the receiving end of the action). Adiaphorizing effects (that is, rendering actions ethically neutral and therefore exempt from ethical evaluation and censure) tend to be achieved these days, however, mostly through replacing 'responsibility *for others*' with 'responsibility *to oneself*' and 'responsibility *for oneself*' rolled into one. The collateral victim of the leap to the consumerist rendition of freedom prevalent in the 'liquid' phase of modernity is the Other as the prime object of ethical responsibility and moral concern.

Faithfully following the convoluted itinerary of the 'public mood' in her widely read and highly influential book a couple of decades ago, Colette Dowling declared the desire to be safe, warm and taken care of to be a 'dangerous feeling'.[11] She warned the Cinderellas of the coming age to beware of falling into the trap: in the impulse to care for others and the desire of being cared for by others looms the awesome danger of dependency, of losing the ability to select the tide presently most comfortable for surfing, and to swiftly move from one wave to another the moment the current changes direction. As Arlie Russell Hochschild comments, 'her fear of being dependent on another person evokes the image of the American cowboy, alone, detached, roaming free with his horse . . . On the ashes of Cinderella, then, rises a postmodern cowgirl.' The most popular of the empathizing/counselling best-sellers of the day 'whisper[ed] to the reader: "Let the emotional investor beware" . . . Dowling cautions women to invest in the self as a solo enterprise.'

> The commercial spirit of intimate life is made up of images that prepare the way for a paradigm of distrust . . . by offering as ideal a self well defended against getting hurt . . . The heroic acts a self can perform . . . are to detach, to leave, and to depend on and need others less . . . In many cool modern books, the author prepares us for people out there who don't need our nurturance and for people who don't or can't nurture us.[12]

The eventualities of populating the world with more caring people and/or inducing people to care more do not figure in the panoramas painted in the consumerist utopia. The privatized utopias of the cowboys and cowgirls of the consumerist era brandish instead a vastly expanded 'free space' (free for *myself*, of course); vast, but also 'gated' space, barred to uninvited and unwelcome visitors; a kind of space of which the liquid modern consumer, bent on solo performances and only on solo performances, always needs more and never has enough. The space which liquid modern consumers need and are advised, nudged and emboldened from all sides to fight for can be gained and owned only by evicting or demeaning other humans – but particularly the kinds of humans who care and/or may need to be cared for.

It is the consumer *market* that has now taken over from solid modern *bureaucracy* the task of adiaphorization: the task of squeezing the nasty fly of 'being *for*' out of the appetizing 'being *with*' ointment. Just as Emmanuel Levinas adumbrated when he mused that 'society', rather than being, as Hobbes suggested, a contraption to make peaceful and friendly human togetherness achievable for *inborn egoists* through cutting down or repressing their selfish inclinations, might be a stratagem to make 'centripetal' concerns and a self-centred, self-referential, egoistic life attainable for *inborn moral beings* by cutting down on the infinite responsibilities for others inevitably triggered by the face of the Other; indeed, by the unavoidable fact of human togetherness.

> It is extremely important to know if society in the current sense of the term is the result of a limitation of the principle that men are predators of one another, or if to the contrary it results from the limitation of the principle that men are *for* one another. Does the social, with its institutions, universal forms and laws, result from limiting the consequences of the war between men, or from limiting the infinity which opens in the ethical relationship of man to man?[13]

The present pressures are not towards self-enclosure and withdrawal from the world. On the contrary, the release of the individual from the tight network of inherited or artificially composed but solidified network of loyalties and obligations has made the liberated individuals *open* to the world out there as never before in human history. That new openness recasts the outside world as a huge container of infinite chances and opportunities which may be gained or lost, enjoyed or bewailed, depending on the individual's skills, ingenuity and effort. As such, the world is simultaneously a site of exciting adventure and a wilderness filled to the brim with dark, horrifying dangers (the danger of failure, with the shame and humiliation it brings, arguably occupying pride of place among them); simultaneously an object of intense curiosity and desire, and a source of terror and the impulse to escape.

All in all, letting loose the centrifugal propulsion portends incalculable risks; but repressing it altogether and exclusively following the centripetal drives wouldn't do either. Neither choice is unambiguously desirable, neither is free from terrifying and repellent side-effects. A compromise between the extremes is not easy to strike, and a trail steering clear of the two similarly off-putting extremes has yet to be blazed. One can say, metaphorically, that a life itinerary needs to oscillate between the equally treacherous temptation and horrors of anorexia and bulimia . . .

Excursus: Eating as an archetype of life choices   The shelf-life of best-selling books in bookstores is nowadays somewhere between milk and yoghurt; the titles on the bestseller lists change from one week to another. And yet two kinds of books appear, in the US at least, on every or almost every weekly list. These are the books on new dieting regimes, and cookbooks with new exciting and whimsical food recipes.

The American (and not just the American) soul is split. Trained, prodded and counselled to seek ever new pleasures, while exposed daily to ever new promises and temptations, Americans (and not only Americans) yearn for raptures of the palate as yet untried, as well as for being watched and admired (don't forget the ego-boosting craving!) in the role of refined and sophisticated gourmets or connoisseurs by friends, the style police, style vigilantes and other people who count. Trained, prodded and counselled to keep their bodies, those receptacles of past, present and hopefully future pleasures, fit to go on absorbing new delights, but warned daily against fat, toxicants and other 'enemies within' which threaten to prevent them from doing so if they are allowed to get in, Americans (and not just Americans) can only watch with suspicion every morsel of food they put in their mouths, count the calories that would need to be disposed of were the morsels ingested, and study the strange chemical terms on food packages in the hope of striking the right balance between the hoped-for benefits and possible harms. A double bind, if there ever was one; a classic setting for a split and conflict-ridden personality; in the fashionable (even if hotly contested) medical term – for schizophrenia. Each step taken or contemplated calls for an antidote effacing its morbid side-effects. Viagra in the evening, a contraceptive pill the morning after . . .

Which makes anorexia and its *alter ego* bulimia the twin offspring of the liquid modern life of the consumer. Both (blatantly unidentical) twins are well attuned to a life condemned to endless choices, forcing the artist of life to navigate between incompatible values and contradictory impulses. Whenever the contradiction persists, the efforts made to resolve it, and the knowledge used in those efforts, are bound to be deemed inadequate, and the actor is likely to be accused of ineptitude or neglect.

N. F. Miller and J. Dollard, American psychologists, conducted an experiment with rats faced with a 'package deal' of tasty lard and a nasty electric shock. The rats circled around the source of the ambivalent message, unable to do anything rational (there was hardly anything rational to do . . .). The two researchers developed a theory in 1941: at the point where there is a balance between 'adiance' and 'abiance' (pull and push, attraction and repellence; attraction growing with hunger, repulsion rising with proximity to the bare electric wire), imbalance of mind and irrationality of behaviour are the most likely reactions. Konrad Lorenz experimented with sticklebacks for a change, cramped in an aquarium that was too small for them, so they were unclear as to whether they were still in their own territorial water (in which case instinct would prompt them to fight off intruders) or on the territory of another stickleback (in which case, they would clear off). Facing such contradictory signals, incomprehensible and impossible to reconcile, the fishes turned tails up and buried their heads in the sand, unable to follow either of the two 'rational' patterns: unable to choose between attack and escape.

Both experiments cast some light on the phenomena of anorexia and bulimia in the liquid modern society of consumers, where 'package deals' of attractive gains and abhorred side-effects, as well as ambivalence of the rules ascribed to situations of choice, are common and permanent features. One could even say that under the circumstances anorexia and bulimia are predictable reactions, were it not for one crucial factor absent in rats or fishes: forms assumed by *human* reactions tend to be *culturally* induced, rather than being determined by inborn instincts and so immune to the vagaries of cultural norms. While ambivalence is the constant companion of the human existential condition, human reactions would probably not take the form of food-related disorders were it not for the present-day preponderance of the 'centripetal' drive, and the resulting tendency to identify *le souci de soi* (self-concern) and *l'amour propre* (self-esteem) with, primarily or even exclusively, care of the *body*: more precisely, with the care of bodily *fitness*, that is the ability of the body to produce and absorb the pleasures which can be offered by the world and the other humans populating it, and with the body's *appearance*, intended to attract potential donors of pleasur-able sensations.

Souci de soi reduced (or almost) to the care of the body casts the men and women of the consumerist society in a situation similar to Miller and Dollard's rats and Lorenz's sticklebacks. The borderline between the body and the rest of the world is bound to become the site of intense *ambivalence* and so also acute *anxiety*. The 'world out there' remains the (sole) source of all the substances necessary for bodily survival, as well as supplying the pleasures motivating the care of the body. That world, however, also contains dangers to the survival of the body, and to its pleasure-generating and pleasure-consuming capacity. Awesome dangers – the known ones among them being all the more horrifying for being ubiquitous yet underdefined, and for that reason difficult to spot and to avoid, and the rest of them being still more terrifying for remaining as yet unmet, undisclosed and for that matter invisible. The radical (rational?) solution to the quandary – closing the boundary and prohibiting frontier traffic altogether – is not, however, an option. Secu-rity from toxins can only be increased by surrendering more pleasures, and can be made foolproof only Hades-style: by putting an end to all pleasure and joy. The whole interface between the body and the outer world therefore needs to be closely watched; the apertures of the body need full-time armed guards, 24/7 – and vigilant and strict immigration officers.

Anorexia is an equivalent of the North Korean or Burmese type of response to the ambivalence of the outside world: closing the borders altogether, prohibiting all imports from beyond them, at the price of keeping the insiders in a state of perpetual misery and want. The insiders may even get used to their life of misery and start fearing any change; famished, they will resent the feeling of a full stomach – like the hero of Franz Kafka's story *A Hunger Artist*, outraged and despairing at having his fast limited to only forty days: 'Why stop fasting in this particular moment, after forty days of it? He had held out for a long time, an illimitably long time; why stop now, when he was in his best fasting form, or rather, not yet quite in his best fasting form? Why should he be cheated of the fame he would get for fasting longer . . . since he felt that there were no limits to his capacity of fasting?'[14]

Bulimia, on the other hand, means facing the challenge point-blank and resolving to fight it on its own terms. It can be seen as Gregory Bateson's *symmetrical* variety of 'schismogenetic chain', where both sides in a conflict (market-induced temptations and targeted consumers) compete in the same game with the same weapons and for the same stakes, any triumph of one boosting the resolve and the fighting spirit of the other. The more brazen, impudent and obtrusive the challenge, the more defiant and provocative the response. Opulence answered with more opulence, excess with more excess . . .

To be sure, both responses are *culturally* prompted; spreading like copy-cat behaviour, they are likely to go out of fashion in a similar manner. After all, they are fanciful responses to a genuine problem; irrational, since they neither resolve the problem nor prompt it to go away. Sooner or later, their ineffectiveness is likely to erode their popularity – and new responses, not necessarily more effective but so far untried and not yet discredited, will be sought and found. To cut off the roots from which they grow will take more than that, however. The roots, after all, are sunk and proliferate in the fertile soil of liquid modern consumerist opulence.

Having expanded individual opportunities and prospects for enjoyment, the new openness has thus far failed to render the same service to the perceived responsibilities of individuals for the possibilities and prospects of the world. The metaphor of a 'hunter' fits that tendency well, just as the metaphor of the 'gardener' used to correspond to the dominant socializing pressures and recommended life strategies of the 'solid' phase of the modern era, and the metaphor of 'gamekeeper' used to fit the prevailing trends of premodern times.

Hunters do not spend much time scrubbing, polishing and refurbishing their homes. Hunters are anxious to go *out*; they adore open spaces; it is out there, in the so far unexplored expanses crammed with game and teeming with adventure, that they hope to come across happiness waiting to be discovered. Their way of pursuing happiness leads them into the wide world. Is this, then, the centrifugal force which their desire for happiness releases, and which, once released, keeps hunters on the move? Yes, sort of . . . With one proviso, though. Like the legendary King Midas who turned everything he touched into gold, everything that hunters touch (or see, or expect and hope to see) is transformed into hunted game, or game inviting hunting. The world visited by hunters becomes a hunting ground.

A variety of centrifugal force, then, but not the only one which can be released by the outward-looking pursuit of happiness. All varieties of centrifugal force ultimately rebound on the 'centre', whether by design or default; each variety is triggered by the desire for happiness, and each serves, whether by design or default, the happiness of those by whom it is deployed or whom it guides. In all varieties, the opposition between selfish and altruistic motives is blurred and tends to be effaced altogether. But whereas in the case of the 'being *for* others' variety of centrifugal force the centripetal force can be interpreted as its unanticipated, unintended, out-of-focus side-effect, or an overflow, the centrifugal force that keeps hunters on the move appears to be a consciously selected and zealously pursued staple product of the centripetal impulse; in fact, an extension of its centripetal opposite.

The opposition between centripetal and centrifugal forces bifurcating from the joint stem of the pursuit-of-happiness impulse is not of the 'either–or' kind. Clearly distinguishable solely as abstract models, the two forces seldom appear separately in life practices; an 'and–and' relationship is rather the rule. Nevertheless, they confront the happiness-seeking actor as a genuine *choice*. The salience or near invisibility of the unchosen alternative and the form its presence takes are (conscious or unconscious) consequences of that choice; both stay within the realm of the actor's responsibility.

The rest of this chapter is devoted to the frame inside which that choice between the strategies of the search for happiness is bound to be made, and in which responsibility for its consequences might arise, by design or default, and be (consciously) assumed. Friedrich Nietzsche and Emmanuel Levinas have been selected to act as the spokesmen, for the centripetal and centrifugal poles respectively of the continuum along which the choices are visualized and practices are plotted.

In *Ecce Homo*, a book coming closer than all the rest of his writings to the model of a 'reasoned autobiography' – a public confession of the intended meaning and significance of the author's work ('bearing witness' about himself, in his own words) – Friedrich Nietzsche leaves nothing to his readers' imagination. Bluntly and in no ambiguous terms, he proclaims and deplores the 'disparity between the greatness of [his] task and the smallness of [his] contemporaries', manifested in the fact that he has been 'neither heard nor even so much as seen'.

These words, let us note, were put to paper in the autumn of 1888; Nietzsche would hardly have been able to lodge a similar complaint 120 years later, in a society that had evidently 'matured' enough to listen, and to look, and to like what it heard when it listened, and what it saw when it looked – a society which Nietzsche supplied *avant la lettre* with the vocabulary it found suited to narrating its own mood and intentions. What Nietzsche suggested in 1888 – 'Only the day after tomorrow belongs to me. Some are born posthumously'[15] – proved itself destined to come true. Evidently not trusting his contemporaries to direct their eyes and ears to where his greatness waited to be discovered, Nietzsche announced, just a couple of pages later, that with *Also sprach Zarathustra*, the most outstanding among his books ('the most exalted book that exists', 'also the profoundest', 'the inexhaustible well into which no bucket descends without coming up filled with gold and goodness'), he had given mankind 'the greatest gift that has ever been given it.' And he concluded the retrospective survey of his life with the following verdict:

> I know my fate. One day there will be associated with my name the recollection of something frightful – of a crisis like no other before on earth, of the profoundest collision of conscience, of a decision evoked *against* everything that until then has been believed in, demanded, sanctified. I am not a man, I am dynamite . . .
>
> It is my fate to be the first *decent* human being . . . I was the first to discover the truth . . .[16]

So what was that 'greatest truth' that Nietzsche insisted on having discovered? And why was its discovery anticipated to usher mankind into a crisis never before confronted, let alone lived through? Nietzsche's discovery, in his opinion, was that morality is a sham, a sign of decadence, and the product of a conspiracy of the weak and indolent, cowardly and inept, against all that is great and noble and sublime and powerful and inspired and worthy of pride ('it is only among *decadents* that *pity* is called a virtue'). To define himself, Nietzsche chose the word 'immoralist': 'I am proud to possess this word which sets me off against the whole of humanity.'[17]

And immoralist he was, vociferously defying and contemptuously rejecting, wholesale, the Judeo-Christian lore of ethical teaching on which the formation called 'European civilization' (more exactly, its self-understanding and – endlessly pursued though never fully reached – ideal) was founded. He turned upside down the axioms on which the idea of morality, of the opposition between good and evil, rested.

> What is good? All that enhances the feeling of power . . .
> What is bad? All that proceeds from weakness . . . The weak and the botched shall perish: first principle of our humanity. And they ought even to be helped to perish.
> What is more harmful than any vice? – Practical sympathy with all the botched and weak . . .[18]

'I know joy in destruction', Nietzsche admitted, proudly. 'I am therewith *destroyer par excellence*.'[19] Several generations of other 'destroyers par excellence', armed with weapons suited to make the words flesh (and more to the point, to make the words *kill* the flesh), who worked hard to make Nietzsche's vision a reality, could draw inspiration from him – and many among them did. What they could learn from Nietzsche – and embraced most avidly – was praise of the 'pathos of distance',[20] of the 'aristocratic attitude of mind' that 'has been most thoroughly undermined by the lie of the equality of souls'. They could find absolution for their intention of 'helping the weak and the botched to perish' in Nietzsche's verdict that the ethics bequeathed by Christianity to his contemporaries (by whose 'foul breath' he felt 'asphyxiated') was 'the revolt of all things that crawl on their bellies against everything that is lofty.'[21] That Christian ethics was the poisonous relic of the revolt of 'stealthy canker-worms', a 'cowardly, effeminate and sugary gang' . . .

Humankind, for Nietzsche, was split into two categories: the powerful and *therefore* perfect ('therefore' since 'the idea of political superiority always resolves itself into the idea of psychological superiority' – for instance, 'clean' and 'unclean' 'confront each other for the first time as badges of class distinction'[22]); and the weak and *therefore* botched. This fundamental division overrides in his view all other divisions and serves as their ultimate explanation. The powerful are

> the aristocratic, the high-stationed, the high-minded, who have felt that they themselves were good, that is to say of the first order, in contradistinction to all the low, the low-minded, the vulgar, the plebeian . . . The pathos of nobility and distance . . . the chronic

and despotic *esprit de corps* and fundamental instinct of a higher dominant race coming into association with a meaner race, an 'under race', this is the origin of the antithesis of good and bad.

And how does it happen that the 'aristocratic and powerful' become the yardstick, and indeed a synonym, of everything good and noble, while the rest turn into a meaner 'under race', the vulgar and the plebeian? Well, 'the masters' right of giving names goes so far that it is permissible to look upon language itself as an expression of the power of the masters . . .' The powerful *have* that right to 'seal others in words' of their choice because they *can* do it; because *only* they, the powerful, can. It is against this fundamental truth that the ethics invented by Judaism and taken over and expanded by Christianity was a rebellion – a rebellion, we may understand, of those 'sealed in words' and sealed off from the universe of goodness. On the banners of rebellion, a reversal of the truth was embroidered:

> the wretched are alone the good; the poor, the sick, the loathsome, are the only ones that are pious, the only ones that are blessed, for them alone is salvation – but you, on the other hand, you aristocrats, you men of power, you are to all eternity the evil, the horrible, the covetous, the insatiate, the godless; eternally also shall you be the unblessed, the cursed, the damned![23]

That rebellion was born of envy called *ressentiment*, that peculiar blend of jealousy, envy and cognitive dissonance; it needed no other source, and so needs no other explanation. Rebellion was and remains an act of vengeance for the higher and nobler quality of the powerful; not for the unjust, selfish uses they make of their power, as the spokesmen of the rebels would aver. That rebellion was and remains a revenge for high-mindedness, not high-handedness . . . The inferior could not bear the sight of their betters; they found that sight humiliating and revolting, since what they saw was simultaneously coveted and unachievable, hotly desired yet forbidden to them. They suspected an inevitability of failure in the event that they were to try to match the splendours of their betters. What came to their betters naturally, matter-of-factly, could come to them only as an artifice, as violence perpetrated on nature; but the way of being-in-the-world they envied in their betters while coveting it for themselves was precisely the *impossibility* of artifice – all and any artifice, imitation, copying. Once passed over to, or stolen by, inferiors, the 'good' of the superiors could not but turn into evil, its opposite. The expropriation of the lords, so Nietzsche insisted, wouldn't – couldn't – ennoble the commons.

> The 'well-born' simply *felt* themselves 'happy'; they did not have to manufacture their happiness artificially through looking at their enemies, or in cases to talk and lie themselves into happiness (as is the custom with all resentful men); and similarly, complete men as they were, exuberant with strength, and consequently *necessarily* energetic, they were too wise to dissociate happiness from action . . .
>
> [A]ll in sharp contrast to the 'happiness' of the weak and the oppressed, with their festering venom and malignity, among whom happiness appears essentially as a narcotic, a deadening, a quietude, a peace, a 'Sabbath', an enervation of the mind and relaxation of the limbs – in short, a purely *passive* phenomenon.[24]

Unlike more reticent because politically correct (read: hypocritical) defenders of the universal benefits of inequality, Nietzsche does not soften the bluntness of his advocacy of aristocratic order by adumbrating/anticipating/promising the 'trickle-down' effect: happiness is the *exclusive* domain of the superior few, and the only good the plebeians may reasonably expect to derive out of that exclusivity can be drawn from acceptance of this law of nature. Accepting it, they will spare themselves the trials and tribulations, torments and frustrations which their *ressentiment* would inevitably inflict.

We may say that the wisdom of aristocratic order lay, in Nietzsche's view, in giving to all what can reasonably be theirs: the happiness of exuberance to the strong, the tranquillity of meekness and the placid acceptance of fate to the weak. Pity and compassion for the weak and hapless are in that view as cruel as they are ineffective: they won't make the weak stronger, only unhappy; the imprudently awakened hopes will only add the insult of defeat to the injury of inferiority. As Zarathustra, Nietzsche's authorized spokesman and plenipotentiary, puts it: 'My greatest danger always lay in indulgence and sufferance; and all humankind wants to be indulged and suffered.'[25] The selfishness of the great and mighty is 'healthy and holy' since their very greatness and might is a gift (the only gift, but the greatest and most generous imaginable) to all humankind. Alas, Zarathustra would say, there is also another selfishness, the selfishness of those who have only their weakness and baseness to offer; a sick selfishness, 'an all-too-poor, a hungry selfishness that always wants to steal . . . It looks with the eye of a thief upon all lustrous things; with the greed of hunger it measures him who has plenty to eat; and it is always skulking about the table of the givers.'[26]

The message of Zarathustra, Nietzsche's mouthpiece, is anything but recondite or ambiguous. There is happiness for *everybody*, but not *the same* happiness for each. The 'healthy and holy' selfishness of the high and mighty, noble and strong-willed, *is* happiness – whereas the sole 'happiness' (more correctly, the avoidance of unhappiness) to be attained by the rest is to take that redoubtable truth in, and abide by what it tells them; above all, to accept their own mediocrity and promptly abandon their fanciful dreams – and so refrain from abortive actions which they, albeit only to their own detriment, mistakenly expect to make them like those above them, though they *are not* them and can never *become* them.

There is no room in that picture for the *pursuit* of happiness. Each of the two starkly different variants of 'happiness' is a quality which one can't *obtain*: one either has it or doesn't – though it can still be forfeited, if one allows oneself to be deceived by the siren songs of compassion (in the case of the high and mighty) or *ressentiment* (in the case of the vulgar and lowly). The verdicts of Nature can be tinkered with only at the tinkerers' peril. To avoid ruin, humans must be freed: the high and mighty from pity, compassion, (unjustly) guilty consciences and (uncalled for) *scruples* – and the vulgar and lowly from *hope*.

Much has been written in commentary on Nietzsche's portrayal of the *Übermensch*, a man called to great things and ready to follow his calling. That man is not promised an easy life: he must first win his freedom and then defend it with all his might. He is the only type in Nietzsche's split-in-the-middle panorama of humans who may be called a 'self-made man' – who, indeed, must *become* what he *is*: deploy the powers of the Superman and resolve to fulfil his vocation as the Superman and reach the Superman's identity. The odds against fulfilment are made to the measure of his supreme powers and unwavering will. The odds again are the crowds of 'small people' . . .

In a chapter entitled 'On the virtue that makes small', Zarathustra shares with his listeners the Superman's emotions:

> I go among this people and keep my eyes open . . . They peck at me because I tell them: For small people small virtues are necessary – and because it is hard for me to understand that small people are *necessary*! . . .
>
> I go among this people and keep my eyes open: they have become *smaller* and are becoming even smaller: *and their doctrine of happiness and virtue is the cause*. . . .
>
> Fundamentally they want one thing most of all: that nobody shall do them harm. So they steal a march on everyone and do good to everyone.
>
> This, however, is *cowardice*: although it be called 'virtue' . . .
>
> They are clever, their virtues have clever fingers, but they lack fists, their fingers do not know how to fold into fists. . . .
>
> This, however, is – *mediocrity*: although it be called moderation . . .
>
> You will become smaller and smaller, you small people! You will crumble away, you comfortable people! You will yet perish – through your many small virtues, through your many small omissions, through your many small submissions![27]

Words like this, dripping with contempt for the 'small people', can be heard again falling from the lips of Harry Lime, the unscrupulous wartime profiteer in Carol Reed's film *The Third Man*, at the top of the Ferris wheel of the Viennese Prater, 64.75 metres up. From that height, people do look small and insignificant – more like ants or cockroaches than humans. Harry Lime could therefore view their agonies and deaths, caused by penicillin adulterated for the greater profit of illicit traders, as just 'collateral damage', not counting for much and hardly ever counted; as that 'nothing' unworthy of much ado. 'Small people' are not quite the kind of humans to which the treatment owed to humans is due. Especially from that other human at the top of the Ferris wheel of fortune.

They may be small (they are!), but there are many of them; they, Nietzsche spells it out through the lips of Zarathustra, 'become a hindrance to anyone who is in a hurry'. There is 'as much weakness as justice and pity'. Justice and pity *are* weaknesses. To be just and to pity means being weak. Power means the *rejection* of pity – and of justice. At least justice as the 'small people' would have it: 'The mob blink and say: "We are all equal" . . . "There are no Higher Men, we are all equal, man is but man, before God – we are all equal!" . . . But now this God has died. And let us not be equal before the mob . . . You Higher Men, this God was your greatest danger . . . God has died: Now we desire – that the Superman shall live.'[28]

It was the coming of the Superman that made God redundant. With indulgence, sufferance and pity swept out of the way, in the world as seen (adumbrated, anticipated, augured, desired and ushered) by the Higher Man, there is no room for God – that God of equality and the patron of the *preservation* of man . . . In that coming world of the Higher Man, the challenge is no longer how to preserve man, but 'how shall man be overcome?'[29]

Nietzsche's most often repeated demand is for a 'revaluation of all values'. Given pride of place among the values most urgently needing to be revalued are compassion and pity for the weaker. Weakness is sin, and is not to be pitied, but treated with contempt and no mercy. Liberation means shattering the shackles of compassion. By definition, therefore, freedom is a proposition for the few, for the Higher Men (current or aspiring), and for freedom to be achieved by the few, the rest – the 'small people' – need to be freed from (read: stripped of) their illusions of equality and of a right to compassion.

Nietzsche's frankness in expounding the creed of the practitioners of the centripetal variety of the pursuit of happiness as practised by 'postmodern cowgirls' and 'postmodern cowboys' was unpalatable to *his* contemporaries; no wonder he considered himself a 'forerunner'. Since then, however, his sincerity has turned from a liability into his major asset. The Harry Limes of the liquid modern time of consumers may quote Nietzsche and so avoid charges of political incorrectness, avoid putting their own name to it and causing public outrage; this is perhaps the main, though not necessarily the most advertised, cause of Nietzsche's present-day popularity. Ours is the time of Nietzsche's resurrection. No longer viewed as iconoclast and/or curiosity, he is valued by many present-day interpreters as a most, and arguably *the* most, perceptive spokesman for the emotions that set in motion and guide the life philosophy of a growing number of *our* contemporaries.

If the *Übermensch* (the 'Higher Man' or 'Superman') may be singled out as the axial category around which the philosophy of Friedrich Nietzsche rotates, it is the category of *responsibility* that provides the focus for Emmanuel Levinas's work. Juxtaposed, these two categories imply and convey the polarity of the opposition between the two teachings when they are seen as life philosophies. The first suggests a programme of ego care, ego enhancement and altogether *self-referential* concerns; it also presents the pursuit of happiness as an effort in self-promotion. The second offers a prospect of care and concern for the Other – and the happiness of 'being *for*'.

According to Emmanuel Levinas, it is the responsibility for the Other that is the 'essential, primary and fundamental structure' of my subjectivity. Ethics, the impulse of moral duty, the urge to act on my own responsibility, are not the icing on the cake of my being, not supplements to being, or desirable but not necessary adornments of my existence; it is rather that 'the very node of the subjective is knotted in ethics understood as responsibility'.[30] *I am because I am for others*. For all practical intents and purposes, 'being' and 'being for other' are synonyms.

The Face of the Other when it enters/bursts into my sight beckons to me, opening the possibility of escape from 'the isolation of existing' – and thereby calls me into *being*, which unlike mere 'existence' is inconceivable without sharing ('existence', Levinas reminds us, 'is the sole thing I cannot communicate; I can tell about it, but I cannot share my existence').[31] It is from the responsibilities I carry that my 'self' is woven: responsibilities 'for what is not my deed, or for what even does not matter to me'. 'Since the Other looks at me, I am responsible for him, without even having *taken* on responsibilities in his regard.' 'The face orders and ordains me.'[32] Ordains through ordering, orders through ordaining . . .

Responsibility so understood precedes, we may say, all intentionality on my part. It also bears no relevance to our relationship conceived as my dependence on him or his on me. In the phrase 'the face orders me', the verb 'orders' is used metaphorically. It does not refer to 'ordering' in its ordinary, vernacular sense – as giving a command to be obediently followed. That other whose 'face' orders me into responsibility is *not* my superior, not a boss who could inflict pain or otherwise punish me for neglecting the command or refusing to fulfil it. If I obey the order, it is not because of the Other's superior power but because of his or her weakness, her or his inability to coerce me into taking on that responsibility which has become mine with his or her presence; Levinas would say with his or her 'proximity', but the word 'proximity' is, just like the word 'orders', used metaphorically – in the sense neither of *physical* closeness nor *institutional* proximity (such as, for instance, proximity of kinship), but referring solely to the act of *casting me in a state of responsibility.*

As already mentioned above, entering a state of responsibility is not a transaction: not a contract, not an act of spelling out, let alone balancing, our respective rights and duties, promises and expectations.

> Intersubjective relation is not a symmetrical relation . . . I am responsible for the Other without waiting for the reciprocity, were I to die for it. Reciprocity is *his* affair. It is precisely insofar as the relationship between the Other and me is not reciprocal that I am subjection to the Other; and I am 'subject' essentially in this sense. It is I who support all . . . The I always has one responsibility *more* than all the others . . .
>
> It is I who support the Other and am responsible for him . . . My responsibility is untransferable, no one could replace me. In fact, it is a matter of saying the very identity of the human I starting from responsibility . . . Responsibility is what is incumbent on me exclusively, and what, *humanly*, I cannot refuse . . . I am I in the sole measure that I am responsible, a non-interchangeable I. I can substitute myself for everyone, but no one can substitute myself for me. Such is my inalienable identity of subject.[33]

In a variety of contexts and using a variety of wordings, Levinas repeatedly admits and warns that 'an ethical exigency is not an ontological necessity'.[34] Responsibility for an-Other, being *for* the other, is 'real' in a different (one would say *weaker*) sense than *physical* realities or even the reality of '*social* facts', memorably defined by Émile Durkheim as having indomitable coercive power and the penal sanctions to threaten those defying and violating them. Responsibility *has no capacity to determine* my actions.

One can remain blind and deaf to the ethical exigency, or defy it intentionally and in full consciousness, without being brought to a court of law, and with only a moderate or slight risk of ostracism, communal sanctions or irreparable damage to one's self-esteem. Facing up to ethical responsibility, taking on that responsibility, *assuming responsibility for that responsibility*, is a matter of *choice* – having few or no odds in its favour except the voice of conscience. The assumption of responsibility is in no way *guaranteed*; 'there is in the human the possibility to not awake to the Other; there is a possibility of evil ... I have no certainty whatsoever that the "otherwise than being" [this is what Levinas calls submission to the Other – that exit from the loneliness of self-centred being] is bound to triumph.'[35] The odds are even, at best, and all too often militate against the ethical stance. Ethics is not stronger or 'more real' than existence; it is only *better*. Taking responsibility for my responsibility is the outcome of pursuing that 'better' – of a pursuit that may or may not be undertaken ...

This is, ultimately, the choice, the ultimate choice, which we all confront in our pursuit of happiness. A choice that needs to be made daily, and then steadfastly held to while being day in, day out reaffirmed.

We can only repeat the words of Seneca, quoted at the beginning, that 'when it comes to seeing clearly what it is that makes life happy' we 'grope for the light'; and add, two millennia later, that we don't seem to be much closer to that light than Seneca's contemporaries. We continue groping. This is, ultimately, what the 'art of life' is about.

AFTERWORD
On Organizing and Being Organized

So we are all artists of our lives – knowingly or not, willingly or not, like it or not. To be an artist means to give form and shape to what otherwise would be shapeless or formless. To manipulate probabilities. To impose an 'order' on what otherwise would be 'chaos': to 'organize' an otherwise chaotic – random, haphazard and so unpredictable – collection of things and events by making certain events more likely to happen than all the others.

'To organize' (or 'to manage': the two expressions are Siamese twins) means to get things done by bringing together and coordinating various, otherwise separate and scattered actors and resources (tacit assumption: such togetherness and cooperation would not otherwise happen). To express what is involved we often speak of the need to 'get *things* organized' or indeed 'to get *myself* organized' (in which case we refer to life artistry) – and sometimes explain, though always presume, that this is precisely what we must do if we wish 'to get things done'.

Whom should we ask how best to go about organizing things (including ourselves) if not the professionals: people in charge of the entities called 'organizations'? They are, after all, presumed to specialize in making sure that things are done – day in, day out, infallibly – and properly (that is, as intended). This is what they have been doing and aim to do through all their office time. Until recently, as the Oxford English Dictionary testifies, they were busy 'giving (to something) a definite and orderly structure' (tacit assumption: this 'something' would otherwise stay shapeless and disorderly). *Definite* and *orderly* . . . Ever since it entered and settled in the vernacular, and until quite recently, the concept of 'organization' used to make one think of graphs and diagrams, lines of command, departments, time schedules, rule books; of the victory of *order* (that is, of a state in which some events are *made* much more probable than all other events) over *chaos* (that is, over a state in which anything may happen with equal or incalculable probability); of the 'four c's' – continuity, constancy, consistency, coherence; of the primacy of structure over the structured, frame over contents, totality over individuals, managerial objectives over the conduct of the managed.

I said 'until quite recently' because entering organizational headquarters these days, one feels the blowing of winds of change. A few years ago Joseph Pine and James H. Gilmore published a book under the title *The Experience Economy*,[1] a title which – helped no doubt by its Harvard Business School credentials – instantly inflamed the imagination of business and management students, preparing to recast the current mentality of directors and presidents of companies as the new paradigm of organizational studies. In a volume of fascinating studies published by the Copenhagen Business School Press,[2] its editors Daniel Hjorth and Monika Kostera sketched in broad outline and traced in remarkable detail the itinerary leading from the old organizational paradigm centred on 'management' and prioritizing control and efficiency, to the emergent paradigm focused on entrepreneurship and emphasizing 'the most vital characteristics of experience: immediacy, playfulness, subjectivity and performativity'.

Monika Kostera characterized 'managerialism' (now bygone or in rapid, though occasionally resentful and reluctant, retreat) as 'thriving on power and accumulating more and more of it'. First it took power away from workers and office employees, and then, climbing gradually up the authority levels, even from those situated at the highest administrative levels. 'Factories were turned into giant machines . . . where the workers were seen as mere fallible additions to the conveyer belt. Offices soon followed on the same paths . . . ' On the way from managerialism to the 'experience economy', new types of organizations are born, however, 'entrepreneurial, unabashedly eclectic, nonlinear and sometimes blatantly illogical. They are enacted via immediacy, subjectivity, playfulness, and performativity.[3] And so, it seems, the time has arrived to bid farewell to constancy, consistency and coherence. As to continuity, it may appear, if at all, among the results, but it will no longer feature in designs, declared purposes and motives; and when (if) it does appear, it won't necessarily be recorded by the bosses (or the stockbrokers!) on the credit side of the organization . . .

As to the probable social and personal consequences of such radical transformations in the making, the trial continues and the jury is far from reaching a unanimous verdict. Some observers can (and do!) describe the radical overhaul of organizations as a powerful step towards the emancipation and enablement of employees, while others describe it as a move towards an even tighter ensnaring and entanglement of subordinates and bosses alike in a net of work-generated dependencies. Some speak of another remarkable gain in freedom, others of a new, more voracious, merciless and ubiquitous domination; some of a hasty retreat of dehumanizing regimentation and routine, others of an invasion and conquest of the few remaining spaces of autonomy and privacy; some of an imminent restoration and installation of employees' rights to self-management and self-assertion, others of a further advancement in the expropriation of their personal and private qualities, assets and concerns. All these starkly contradictory and apparently incompatible characterizations of the process ring at least partly true; each can muster enough evidence in its favour to resist being dismissed out of hand.

The advent of the 'experience economy' is indeed ambiguous in its consequences. And its ambiguity stubbornly evades resolution. After all, one of the paramount causes of the impression of the ostensible unstoppability of the passage from the 'managerial' to the 'experience' economy seems to be the partial invalidation of all and any resolute judgements, because of the progressive blurring, softening or effacement of the boundaries that once neatly separated self-sustained and autonomous spheres of life and value areas: the workplace from the home, contracted-out time from free time, work from leisure, and indeed business from the family household (whose separation was memorably proclaimed by Max Weber as the birth act of modernity and its declaration of war on everything that was irrelevant to the

goals of organization and unfit to be subordinated to the impersonal logic of organization).

In the era of mobile telephones, laptops and hand-held comput-
ers, there is no excuse for being temporarily out of reach of either
the workplace or the family home – of business duties or family
obligations. Being constantly at the beck and call of business
partners and bosses as much as of family members and friends
becomes not just a possibility, but a duty as much as an inner
urge; the Englishman's home may still be his castle, but its walls
are porous and anything but insulated for sound. All too often
working from home while having fun at the workplace, English
men and women may be excused for no longer being quite sure
which place is the natural habitat of what; what to expect, where
and when to expect it, and where (if anywhere) and when (if ever)
to conclude that the expectations have been frustrated.

Quite a few functions hitherto considered to belong fully to the
domain of the (managed) workplace have now been 'contracted
out' to the 'cooperators' and thereby replaced by market-type
relations (in the style of 'if not fully satisfied, return the commodity to the shop'), or 'subsidiarized' to each employee individually,
thereby shifting responsibility for performance, and the obligation
to bear its consequences, from the shoulders of the bosses on to
those of the employees. The badge of genuine domination is nowadays the facility with which performance of orthodox managerial
tasks is *avoided*, having been shifted sideways or dropped down
in the hierarchy.

Quite a few large areas of the selves or personalities of the
people (directly or indirectly) hired – areas hitherto left out of the
package deal obtained by the employers in 'buying labour' – are
now open to exploitation once the 'empowered' employees have
become self-managing. *Self*-managing employees can be relied
upon to deploy parts of themselves that were off-limits to the
bosses of traditional labour contracts – reaching for resources
their managers could not reach. The newly 'empowered' employees (whether or not renamed 'subcontractors') can also be expected
not to count the hours spent in serving the aims of the employing
company, as well as to control and neutralize those parts of themselves which might potentially be counterproductive or disruptive,
or at least difficult to tame and disable, if they were entrusted to
the rule and direct responsibility of their managers.

The natural habitat and the greenhouses of the 'subjectivity' or 'playfulness' on which the new type of organization rests its hopes were previously located in homes, friendship networks and neighbourhoods: the very sites which the organizations' new voraciousness for the time, energy and emotions of their employees – coupled with the demand for a 'passionate dedication' elicited by an artificially beefed-up state of alert and emergency – tend to marginalize, emaciate and devalue. Instead of harvesting crops grown independently and made 'ready for harvesting' on those traditional sites, organizations now need to take upon themselves the tasks of sowing and laboriously cultivating the qualities they intend to mobilize in order to increase the 'performativity' of their members.

The outcome may well prove to be contrary to what was intended. The intention was to adjust organizations to the conditions of a liquid, fast-changing setting by making them 'lighter'; but to meet new challenges they may become, on the contrary, still 'heavier'. In a constantly rejuvenating world, they may need, as did the ageing witches of fairy tales, ever larger supplies of virgin blood (in the updated version of the friendly or unfriendly, but always enforced, takeovers euphemistically dubbed 'mergers', and the asset-stripping that follows them). Their progress may acquire bulimic features: bouts of devouring interspersed with spasms of vomiting and fits of liposuction, spells of weight-watching frenzy and weekend breaks in health farms. The exact balances of costs and effects are yet to be calculated, but it seems that the rise in the costs related to serving the new needs may well be found to be greater than the savings obtained through contracting out and subsidiarizing some of the functions performed by their old-style predecessors.

Niels Åkerstrøm, professor at the Copenhagen Business School, compares the present situation of the employee in an organization to that of a partner in a contemporary marriage or in a couple living together. Here as there, a state of emergency (a state calling for the mobilization of all resources, rational and emotional alike) tends to be the norm, not an exception. Here as there, a person 'is always in doubt about how much he is loved or not ... One craves confirmation and recognition in the same way one does in marriage ... [T]he question about whether they are part of something or not drives the individual employee's behaviour.'[4]

'The code of love', Åkerstrøm believes, drives the strategy of the 'new type' organization. And so there is no written contract of employment (just as there is no verbal agreement of cohabitation between lovers) which is fixed forever, 'for better or worse' and 'till death do us part'. Partners are kept perpetually *in statu nascendi*, uncertain about the future, constantly in need of proving yet more convincingly that they 'have earned' and 'deserve' the boss's or the partner's sympathy and loyalty. 'Being loved' is never 'sufficiently' earned and confirmed, it remains forever conditional – the condition being a constant supply of ever new evidence of one's ability to perform, to succeed, to be again and again 'one up' on current or potential competitors. The job is never finished, just as the stipulations of love and recognition are never met completely and unconditionally. There is no time to rest on one's laurels: laurels are known to wilt and fade in no time, successes tend to be forgotten a moment after being scored, life in a company is an infinite succession of emergencies . . . This is an exciting and exhausting life; exciting for the adventurous, exhausting for the weak-hearted.

Last though not least, the logic of the *individualistic* version of 'enabling' promoted by the 'experience economy' renders cooperation, mutual commitments and solidarity between workmates not just redundant, but plainly counterproductive. Little can be gained, while a lot may be forfeited, when a solidary stance is taken and emotional bonds and mutual dedication are strengthened as a result. All aspects of the situation (to name only a few, following a list drawn up by Vincent de Gaulejac,[5] the individualization of salaries, the dispersal of shared claims, the abandonment of collective agreements and the weakening of 'specific solidarities') seem to militate against communal solidarity. It is now everyone for herself or himself, with managers creaming off the gains in 'productivity' deriving from what amounts to clamping the letter 't' of solitary on the 'd' of solidary . . .

Niels Åkerstrøm's observation of the tendency to reshape organizations after a pattern akin to love relationships should have referred us to a yet wider transformation, one that probably lies at the foundation of the 'paradigm change': the profound transformation in the role played by human bonds, particularly by love relationships, and more generally by friendship, in the liquid modern setting. By all accounts, their attraction is currently rising to unprecedented heights, but in inverse proportion to their ability to fulfil the role they are hoped and expected to perform – the role that has been and remains the prime cause of their attraction . . .

It is precisely because we are *willing* 'to form deep friendships and companionship', and crave it more strongly and desperately than ever, that our relationships are full of sound and fury, saturated with anxiety and states of perpetual alert. We *are* willing, since friendship bonds are (in Ray Pahl's felicitous and memorable phrase) our sole (social) 'convoy through the turbulent waters' of the liquid modern world. The 'turbulent waters' we need the help of a convoy to brave are the unstable and frail workplaces saturated and poisoned by mutual suspicion and all too often torn asunder by cut-throat competition; our neighbourhoods under constant threat from developers; abundant roads that are nevertheless similarly uncertain and poorly marked in showing the way to a decent life and in signposts to success, coming up and vanishing with no warning; dangers to the safety of our body and possessions too vague to pinpoint, let alone to fight back against; constant pressures to show our mettle and 'prove ourselves' with little help in mustering the resources such a feat would require; successive recommendations of life fashions that are too fast to catch up with so as to stave off the threat of falling behind or being pushed off the track altogether. The helping hand of a reliable, loyal, faithful, 'till-death-do-us-part' friend, a hand that can be relied on to be stretched out promptly and willingly whenever it is needed – what islands offer to potential shipwrecks or oases to those lost in a desert – we need such hands, and wish to have them – the more of them around the better . . .

However . . . However! In our liquid modern surroundings, lifelong loyalty is a blessing alloyed with many a curse. What if the waves change direction, what if new opportunities beckon that will recycle yesterday's reassuring assets into today's menacing liabilities, cherished possessions into off-putting ballast, buoyant lifebelts into lead weights? What if the near and dear is no longer dear but still vexingly near? Hence the anxiety: the fear of losing friends or partners mixed with the fear of being unable to get rid of those of them who are no longer wanted – topped with the fear of finding oneself at the receiving end of the friend's or partner's urge and resolution: 'I need more space'. The 'network' of human

relations ('network': the never ending play of connecting and dis-
connecting) is nowadays a seat of the most harrowing ambivalence. Which confronts the artists of life with a tangle of dilemmas
which cause more confusion than they offer pointers . . .

'Where is the border between the right to personal happiness
and new love, on the one hand, and reckless selfishness that would
break up the family and perhaps damage the children, on the
other?' asks Ivan Klima.[6] Tracing that border precisely may be a
harrowing task, but of one thing we can be sure: wherever that
border lies, it is breached at the moment when the tying and
untying of human bonds are declared morally indifferent, neutral
acts, so that the actors are a priori relieved from responsibility for
the consequences for each other of their acts: from that very same
unconditional responsibility which love promises, for better or
worse, and struggles to build and preserve. 'The creation of a
good and lasting mutual relationship', in a stark opposition to
seeking enjoyment through objects of consumption, 'requires
enormous effort.' What love needs to be compared to, however,
suggests Klima,

> is the creation of a work of art . . . That too requires imagination,
> total concentration, the combining of all aspects of human per-
> sonality, self-sacrifice on the part of the artist, and absolute
> freedom. But most of all, as with artistic creation, love requires
> action, that is, non-routine activity and behaviour, as well as
> constant attention to one's partner's intrinsic nature, an effort to
> comprehend his or her individuality, and respect. And last but not
> least, it needs tolerance, the awareness that one must not impose
> one's outlook or ideals on one's companion or stand in the way of
> the other's happiness.

Love, we need to conclude, abstains from promising an easy road
to happiness and meaning. The 'pure relationship' inspired by
consumerist practices promises that kind of easy life; but by the
same token it renders happiness and meaning hostages to fate.

To cut a long story short: love is not something that can be
found; not an *objet trouvé* or a 'ready-made'. It is something that
always still needs to be *made* anew and remade daily, hourly;
constantly resuscitated, reaffirmed, attended to and cared for. In
line with the growing frailty of human bonds, the unpopularity
of long-term commitments, the stripping away of 'duties' from

'rights' and the avoidance of any obligations except the 'obligations to oneself' ('I owe this to myself', 'I deserve this', etc.), love tends to be viewed as either perfect from the start, or failed – better to be abandoned and replaced by a 'new and improved' specimen, hopefully genuinely perfect. Such love is not expected to survive the first minor squabble, let alone the first serious disagreement and confrontation . . .

Happiness, recalling Kant's diagnosis, is an ideal not of reason but of imagination. He also warned that out of the crooked timber of humanity no straight thing can ever be made. John Stuart Mill seemed to combine both wisdoms in his warning: once you ask yourself whether you are happy, you cease to be so . . . The ancients probably suspected as much but, guided by the principle *dum spiro, spero* (as long as I breathe, I hope), they suggested that without hard work, life would offer nothing to make it worthwhile. Two millennia later, the suggestion seems to have lost none of its topicality.

Notes

Book epigraphs from Epictetus, *The Art of Living*, interpreted by Sharon Lebell, Harper One, 2007, p. 42, and *Seneca: Dialogues and Essays*, trans. John Davie, Oxford University Press, 2007, p. 85.

Introduction

1 Michael Rustin, 'What is wrong with happiness?', *Soundings* (Summer 2007), pp. 67–84.
2 Robert E. Lane, *The Loss of Happiness in Market Democracies*, Yale University Press, 2000.
3 Richard Layard, *Happiness: Lessons from a New Science*, Penguin, 2005.
4 Jean-Claude Michéa, *L'Empire du moindre mal. Essai sur la civilisation libérale*, Climats, 2007, p. 117.
5 See 'English patience', *Observer Magazine*, 21 Oct. 2007.
6 See 'My favourite outfit', *Observer Magazine*, 22 Apr. 2007, p. 39.
7 Stuart Jeffries, 'To have and to hold', *Guardian*, 20 Aug. 2007, pp. 7–9.
8 Friedrich Nietzsche, *The Genealogy of Morals*, trans. Horace B. Samuel, Dover, 2003, p. 11.
9 Ibid., p. 20.
10 See Hanna Buczyńska-Garewicz, *Metafizyczne rozważania o czasie* [Metaphysical Reflections on Time], Universitas, 2003, pp. 50ff.
11 See Douglas Kennedy, *The Pursuit of Happiness*, Arrow, 2002.

1 Miseries of Happiness

1 Ann Rippin, 'The economy of magnificence: organization, excess and legitimacy', *Culture and Organization*, 2 (2007), pp. 115–29.

2 Max Scheler, 'Das Ressentiment im Aufbau der Moralen', in *Gesammelte Werke*, vol. 3, Bern, 1955; here quoted after the Polish edition, *Resentyment i Moralność*, Czytelnik, 1997, p. 49.

3 Ibid., p. 41.

4 Epictetus, *The Art of Living*, interpreted by Sharon Lebell, Harper One, 2007, p. 22.

5 Immanuel Kant, *Grounding for the Metaphysics of Morals*, trans. James W. Ellington, Hackett, 1981, p. 27.

6 See Aristotle, *The Basic Works of Aristotle*, ed. Richard McKeon, Random House, 1941.

7 Darrin McMahon, *The Pursuit of Happiness: A History from the Greeks to the Present*, Allen Lane, 2006, pp. 337ff.

8 Alexis de Tocqueville, *Democracy in America*, trans. George Lawrence, Harper, 1988, vol. 2, p. 538.

9 Ibid.

10 Here translated from the Polish version published by Zysk i S-ka in 1996. For an alternative translation by John Davie, see *Seneca: Dialogues and Essays*, Oxford University Press, 2007, p. 91: 'The highest good is untouched by death. It knows no ending, it tolerates neither excess nor regret; for the upright mind never turns from its course, or succumbs to self-loathing or alters anything, being perfect. But pleasure is extinguished at the very moment it gives delight; it occupies only a small place, and therefore speedily fills it, and, becoming weary, loses its energy after the first assault.'

11 Émile Durkheim, *Selected Writings*, trans. Anthony Giddens, Cambridge University Press, 1972, p. 110.

12 Ibid., pp. 94, 115.

13 See Seneca, *Epistulae Morales ad Lucilium*, trans. by Robin Campbell as *Letters from a Stoic*, Penguin, 2004, p. 65.

14 *Seneca: Dialogues and Essays*, pp. 41, 85.

15 Ibid., p. 134.

16 Ibid., p. 64.

17 Marcus Aurelius, *Meditations*, trans. Martin Hammond, Penguin, 2006, pp. 13, 15, 19.

18 Ibid., p. 65.

19 Ibid., p. 71.

20 Ibid., pp. 36, 80.

21 Pascal, *Pensées*, trans. A. J. Krailsheimer, Penguin, 1968, p. 59.

22   Ibid., pp. 67, 69.
23   Ibid., p. 70.
24   See Max Scheler, 'Ordo amoris', in *Schriften aus dem Nachlass*, I: *Zur Ethik und Erkenntnislehre*, Franke Verlag, 1927; here quoted after David R. Lachterman's translation in Max Scheler, *Selected Philosophical Essays*, Northwestern University Press, 1973, pp. 100–1.
25   Ibid., p. 117.
26   Ibid., p. 113.
27   Ibid., p. 102.
28   Erich Fromm, *The Art of Loving*, Thorsons, 1995, p. 18.
29   Ulrich Beck and Elisabeth Beck-Gernsheim, *The Normal Chaos of Love*, trans. Mark Ritter and Jane Wiebel, Polity, 1995, pp. 3, 13, 53.
30   Ibid., p. 12.
31   B. Ehrenreich and D. English, *For Her Own Good*, Knopf, 1979, p. 276.
32   Gilles Lipovetsky, *L'ère du vide. Essais sur l'individualisme contemporain*, Gallimard, 1993, pp. 327–8.
33   Ibid., p. 316.
34   Christopher Lasch, *Culture of Narcissism*, Warner Books, 1979, p. 43.
35   Ibid., pp. 22, 55, 126.
36   Jean-Claude Kaufmann, *L'invention de soi*, Armand Colin, 2004, p. 188.
37   Hannah Arendt, *La crise de la culture*, Gallimard, 1972, p. 14.
38   Jean-Claude Michéa, *L'Empire du moindre mal. Essai sur la civilisation libérale*, Climats, 2007, p. 27.
39   Leopold von Ranke, *Civil Wars and Monarchy in France*, trans. M. A. Garvey, Bentley, 1852, vol. 1, p. 325, and vol. 2, p. 50.
40   A primary contemporary source quoted by Leopold von Ranke in *The History of the Popes during the Last Four Centuries*, trans. G. R. Dennis, Bell, 1912, vol. 2, p. 219.
41   See Richard Drake, 'Terrorism and consolation of history', *Hedgehog Review*, 2 (2007), pp. 41–53.
42   Michéa, *L'Empire du moindre mal*, p. 197.
43   Jean-Claude Michéa refers here to J. A. W. Gunn's *L'intérêt ne ment jamais. Une maxime politique du XVIIe siècle*, PUF, 1998, pp. 192, 207.

2   We, the Artists of Life

1   See her conversation with Joanna Sokolińska in 'Wysokie obcasy', *Gazeta Wyborcza*, 6 Nov. 2006.

2 Paul Ricoeur, *Soi-même comme un autre*, Seuil, 1990, p. 210.
3 Michel Foucault, 'On the genealogy of ethics: an overview of work in progress', in *The Foucault Reader*, ed. Paul Rabinow, Random House, 1984, p. 350.
4 Susan Neiman, *Evil in Modern Thought*, Princeton University Press, 2002, pp. 4–5.
5 See *Guardian Weekend*, 4 and 11 Aug. 2007.
6 See Ernst Kris and Otto Kunz, *Legend, Myth and Magic in the Image of the Artist*, trans. Alistair Lang and Lottie M. Newman, Yale University Press, 1979, p. 113.
7 Richard Wray, 'How one year's digital output would fill 161 bn iPods', *Guardian*, 6 Mar. 2007.
8 See 'A bigger bang', *Guardian Weekend*, 4 Nov. 2006.
9 Loïc Wacquant, 'Territorial stigmatization in the age of advanced marginality', *Thesis Eleven* (Nov. 2007), pp. 66–77.
10 Alexander Nehamas, *The Art of Living: Socratic Reflections from Plato to Foucault*, University of California Press, 1998, pp. 10ff.
11 Tzvetan Todorov, *Les Aventuriers de l'Absolu*, Robert Laffont, 2006, pp. 244–8.
12 François de Singly, *Les uns avec les autres. Quand individualisme crée du lien*, Armand Colin, 2003, pp. 108–9.
13 See Claude Dubar, *La Socialisation. Construction des identités sociales et professionelles*, Armand Colin, 1991, p. 113.
14 De Singly, *Les uns avec les autres*, p. 108.
15 Jean-Claude Kaufmann, *L'invention de soi. Une théorie d'identité*, Hachette, 2004, p. 214.
16 Ibid., pp. 212–13.
17 Quoted from Elaine Sciolino, 'New leaders say pensive French think too much', *New York Times*, 22 July 2007.
18 Dennis Smith, *Globalization: The Hidden Agenda*, Polity, 2006, p. 38.
19 Ibid., p. 37.

3   The Choice

1 See Russell Jacoby, *Picture Imperfect: Utopian Thought for an Anti-Utopian Age*, Columbia University Press, 2005, p. 148.
2 Lawrence Grossberg, 'Affect and postmodernity in the struggle over "American modernity"', in *Postmodernism: What Moment?* ed. Pelagia Goulimari, Manchester University Press, 2007, pp. 176–201.
3 Nechama Tec, *When Light Pierced the Darkness*, Oxford University Press, 1987.
4 Quoted from *Guardian Review*, 3 Sept. 2005.

5   See Richard Rorty, 'Honest mistakes', in *Philosophy as Cultural Politics*, Cambridge University Press, 2007, p. 57; Christopher Hitchens, *Why Orwell Matters*, Basic Books, 2002.

6   Knud Løgstrup, *After the Ethical Demand*, trans. Susan Dew and Kees van Kooten Niekerk, Aarhus University, 2002, p. 26.

7   Stephen Toulmin, *The Place of Reason in Ethics*, Cambridge University Press, 1953, p. 146.

8   Knud Løgstrup, *Beyond the Ethical Demand*, University of Notre Dame Press, 2007, p. 105.

9   See Emmanuel Levinas, *Ethics and Infinity: Conversations with Philippe Nemo*, trans. Richard A. Cohen, Duquesne University Press, 1985, pp. 10–11.

10 'Adiaphoric', a term borrowed from the language of the medieval Christian Church, originally meant a belief that was 'neutral' or 'indifferent' in the matters of religious doctrine. Here, in our metaphorical use, 'adiaphoric' means amoral: subject to no moral judgement, having no moral significance.

11 Colette Dowling, *Cinderella Complex*, PocketBook, 1991.

12 See Arlie Russell Hochschild, *The Commercialization of Intimate Life*, University of California Press, 2003, pp. 21ff.

13 Levinas, *Ethics and Infinity*, p. 80.

14 Franz Kafka, 'A Hunger Artist', trans. Willa Main and Edwin Muir, in *Collected Short Stories*, Penguin, 1988, p. 271.

15 Friedrich Nietzsche, *The Antichrist*, trans. Anthony M. Ludovici, Prometheus Books, 2000, p. 1.

16 Friedrich Nietzsche, *Ecce Homo*, trans. R. J. Hollingdale, Penguin, 2004, pp. 5, 96–7.

17 Ibid., pp. 13, 101.

18 Nietzsche, *The Antrichrist*, p. 4.

19 Nietzsche, *Ecce Homo*, p. 97.

20 Nietzsche, *The Antichrist*, p. 63.

21 Ibid., pp. 52, 63.

22 Friedrich Nietzsche, *The Genealogy of Morals*, trans. Horace B. Samuel, Dover, 2003, p. 15.

23 Ibid., pp. 11, 17.

24 Ibid., pp. 20–1.

25 Friedrich Nietzsche, *Thus Spoke Zarathustra*, trans. R. J. Hollingdale, Penguin, 2003, p. 204.

26 Ibid., p. 100.

27 Ibid., pp. 188–91.

28 Ibid., pp. 189, 204, 189, 297.

29 Ibid., p. 297.

30 Levinas, *Ethics and Infinity*, p. 95.

31 Ibid., p. 57.
32 Ibid., pp. 57, 96–7.
33 Ibid., pp. 98–101.
34 This wording appears ibid., p. 87.
35 Emmanuel Levinas, *Entre nous. Essais sur le penser-à-l'autre*, Bernard Grasset, 1991, p. 132.

Afterword

1 B. J. Pine and J. H. Gilmore, *The Experience Economy: Work is Theatre and Every Business is a Stage*, Harvard Business School Press, 1999.
2 Daniel Hjorth and Monika Kostera (eds), *Entrepreneurship and Experience Economy*, Copenhagen Business School Press, 2007.
3 Ibid., pp. 287, 289.
4 Sophie Bjerg Kirketerp, 'The loving organization', *Fo*, 3 (2007) ('The virtual living' issue), pp. 58–9.
5 See Vincent de Gaulejac, *La société malade de la gestion*, Seuil, 2005, p. 34.
6 Ivan Klima, *Between Security and Insecurity*, Thames and Hudson, 1999, pp. 60–2.

Index